free spirit

*The more I look at the world, the more I
see myself in every living thing. Everything
is an aspect of me.*

Emily!
keep on leading
with that
epic spirit
of yours.

Adera

ADERA ANGELUCCI

FREE SPIRIT

For more information visit www.aderaangelucci.com

ADERA ANGELUCCI

Cover Design: Flying Horse Design Studio
Copy Editing: Salvo Communications
Publisher: STOKE Publishing
Book Cover Photos: Claire Ponsford

"Changing lives one chapter at a time! Every woman needs a copy of this golden book of life-changing brilliance, inner guidance and wisdom! Adera's story is a fabulous read, and it will naturally guide you to reflect on your own personal story. *Free Spirit* is empowering!"- **Leesa McGregor, Author of A New Alphabet For Humanity**

"This book is 'Bridget Jones's Diary' meets 'Eat Pray Love,' with a healthy dose of self-helpery on the side! I laughed (and cried!) as Adera traced her journey from 'freak flag flyer' to *Free Spirit.*" - **Shirley Weir, Menopause Chicks**

"*Free Spirit* was an absolute delight to read. Adera's storytelling ability is very compelling and the self reflective questions at the end of each chapter had me thinking about my own story with an inspiration to share it. If you're looking for a book to entertain and enliven your spirit, this one will do just that!" - **Shelly Lynn Hughes, Fresh Magazine**

"Reading *Free Spirit* is like hanging out with a BFF and a bottle of wine, laughing over her wild antics and gutsy moves. Then, becoming amazed as her story of growth and wisdom unfolds. Adera Angelucci is truly a free spirit, and her tale is honest, hilarious, and inspiring. Read this book, and you will want to dance off a cliff then soar with the wind as she does, again and again." - **Bryony Lake, In The Company Of Fairies**

"Adera's dharma is to lift others up. She has a gift of seeing the positive power of relationships and how those might be utilized to make the world a better place. *Free Spirit* is the journey of owning your gifts so you can light up your life and the world. Adera is a true light leader." - **Jay Suttonbrown, Manipura Yoga College**

"Adera inspires me to open doors I didn't know were closed. She offers opportunities to explore breaking out of the caged confinements of comfort or imposed limitations. She encourages each of us to risk being ourselves, knowing that we don't need to go it alone and it's ok to ask for help. As I watch her stand in her own strength, she invites me to stand in mine, as we enjoy life adventures together. I appreciated the raw, vulnerable, chaos to creativity that evolved in this read." - **Karen Angelucci (Mom), Birthright Investment**

CONTENTS

Author's Intention   vii

Prologue   1
A Note Before Continuing   5
1. A Light Is Born   7
2. Love: The Greatest Superpower In The Universe   17
3. Let The Adventures Begin   31
4. Leaning Into Myself   47
5. Ireland   59
6. Landing   69
7. Fuck Me, There He Is   81
8. Relationship   95
9. Leading With Purpose   105
10. Business Is Spiritual. So Is Everything Else.   117

Meet Adera   127
Appreciation   129

AUTHOR'S INTENTION

The idea of writing a book about my life-changing experience living in Ireland has been on my mind for the past twelve years. Every year, I'd sit down to write, get a few sentences in and totally lose the rhythm and excitement for the content. I was gifted something very profound during my stay there, and I wanted to share it with the world but the words weren't able to hit the page. The years went by, and then I misplaced the journal I wrote while I was there, highlighting the events and experiences I went through with the real-time emotions attached, which would have been extremely helpful in the writing process.

Has that ever happened to you? Have you ever not taken action on something that was really important to you?

And now the moment seems lost.

That maybe you missed out? That your chance is gone?

Well, one of the main take-aways in this book is about how it's never too late to take action. If something is important to you, then you must listen and give yourself permission to experience it. You can make new choices for your life right now that uncover purpose and meaning unique to you. For you.

It's been over a decade since my trip to Ireland and I have so much more now to share, so much more to give, so much more to say.

What if the experience of writing this book wasn't meant to happen before now?

What if NOW is the richest, sweetest time to do what YOU have in your heart to do?

What if NOW is the time to let yourself be free to share, to say what it is you feel you need to say?

To set your spirit free?

My hope is this book inspires you to share, to be brave and to carve out your own life adventure.

Love

Adera

PROLOGUE

When I was ten years old, I would often walk by an old dog in my neighbourhood that was stuck in a 10x10 foot cage 24/7. Her owners didn't have the time or desire to take her for walks. Each time I walked by, we would lock eyes. The dog always seemed to be saying, "Please let me out."

A month went by until I had the courage to talk to the owners and ask if I could take her out for a walk after school. They said she'd be hard to handle as she didn't know how to be on a leash. She was a heavy black mutt whose weight equaled my own. I'd never had a dog before, but somehow, I had the confidence that I could handle her. So, they trusted me to take her out.

I stepped into her cage, and she was so excited to see me she almost knocked me over. I knew this wasn't going to be easy. She was hardly controllable. The minute the leash was on and the door was open we were off, her running at the speed of sound and me trying to hold her back. The leash was choking her so much she could hardly breathe. Her continuous gasping for air and coughing made me wonder if this was a good idea. She might have been better off in her cage. At least she wouldn't be hurting herself.

I kept talking to her throughout our walk, assuring her that I wanted to take her out again. That this wasn't going to be her one and only time out of her cage. That she could relax. That I didn't want to hurt her and to please stop pulling so hard.

She didn't listen.

Fifteen minutes later, I had to bring her back. My arms were sore from pulling and I couldn't bear to hear her wheezing any longer. When we returned, the owners gave me a look of *"I told you so, she's just better off in her cage."*

But when I looked at her, she had eyes that said, "That was the most exhilarating thing I have ever done in my life. Thank you."

I knew I had to take her out again.

The next day after school, I came by her cage and she was beaming with excitement. I leashed her up and she started pulling me around the block. This happened about four more times, and then she loosened up a bit.

Within a few weeks, she and I had settled into a manageable groove. We'd become gal pals. She was walking beside me and even sitting and staying. The owners couldn't believe it. But I could. I'd seen her potential the minute I laid eyes on her.

After a few months of our daily walks, I felt confident enough to try her off leash for a game of fetch at a nearby field. She was getting the hang of bringing the ball back and listening to me. I was so proud of her and how far she had come. Suddenly, a couple of kids from school rode onto the field with their bikes. They were going to cut across the highway through a hidden hole in the fence. The dog got excited and chased after their bikes. I ran after her, yelling for her to come back, but it was too late.

I'll never forget the terrifying sound of shrieking brakes. In one horrific moment, she was gone.

I was devastated. How was I going to tell the owners I had just killed their dog? How could I be so irresponsible, just letting her off her leash to play like that? *This is all my fault.* I ran to their house weeping, my heart weighing heavy. We all got in the car and went to find her on the side of the highway.

I'll never forget that day or that dog. I'll never forget seeing that raw potential inside of her waiting to be recognized. I'll never forget the look on her face when she walked beside me with pride. And I'll never forget the hugs, smiles and tail wags for giving her the permission to be free.

I had to find some ounce of peace in knowing that her last few months of life were full of joy. We either depart from this world safely in our man-made cages or we break free and take a huge risk. Either way, one day, we'll leave it a changed place.

The book you're about to read is a memoir of my journey towards living as my true self by forging my own brand of spiritual entrepreneurship. As you'll read, that journey has gone hand in hand with embracing my own unpredictable, risky, and occasionally tragic free-spiritedness. By taking the road less traveled—in other words, the messiest, most questionable road I could find at times—I ended up firmly planted in a life, a marriage, a business, and a way of being that I love.

I should make one thing clear: this book is about me, but it's also about you. I know there are far too many people, especially entrepreneurs, who are struggling with how to embrace their authentic selves, their true purposes. I wouldn't have written this book unless I thought it could bring comfort, inspiration, and yes, plenty of comic relief, to people like you. People trying to free themselves from cages.

Eventually, when I thought back to the beautiful times I'd spent with my canine friend when I was ten years old, I felt that the risk we took had been worth it. Those months of play, freedom, fun, and companionship had been well worth the shock of loss.

That dog's name was Spirit.

This book is a tribute to her and all the other caged souls seizing their chance to be free.

A NOTE BEFORE CONTINUING

At the end of each chapter, you'll find a *"Questions To Free Your Spirit"* section. My hope is that after reading my story you'll venture into uncovering yours. This book is meant to be an inquisitive adventure for you that will gradually help you to nail down your purpose. You're probably already great at asking yourself questions, so this won't be so hard. If you have a journal handy, you can write your answers down. If you don't, I recommend starting one for this process. It's going to be fun to see where this book takes you in freeing your own spirit.

1

A LIGHT IS BORN

*Pushed out of darkness into a blinding new world of light to learn all
you've come here to know is no small quest.*

Wow. You made it. You arrived from the unknowing abyss between
nothing and everything with seemingly little effort on your part.
How mind-blowing is that? Someone must have wanted you here.
But *why*? For what *purpose*?

These have been my big questions for most of my life. For years,
I've sought out mentors and teachers to help me uncover the big
mysteries of life. I've looked to horoscopes, numerology, spirit-
guides, psychics and healers. Curiosity about the truth of who I am
and why I am here has compelled me to look outside of myself for
clues.

I've also always had an inner dialogue that speaks to me like a
friendly outsider. It says things like, "Oh, this is what this person
thinks you should do; what do you think?" Or, "Wow, did you see
that? That person just looked at you and gave zero shits!" Or, "This
decision doesn't seem wise, are you sure you want to do this?"

I get that I'm talking to myself. Yet it feels like it's coming from somewhere else, like a separate source that I hear.

In these pages, I'll be sharing my journey of beginning to trust that voice above all others. I'll tell the stories of how I got to know my own free spirit firsthand. I'll also show how I tapped into my unique purpose, my self-love and my reason for being here.

Do you ask yourself big questions and look for answers in guides and mentors? My hope is that this book will be your faithful companion as you start to pay attention to your own unique light within.

Your light is your spirit. And whether or not you choose to listen to it and act on it, your time here will one day end. It's how you choose to live out your life that truly matters. Will you stay stuck in your cage or break free to experience *you* in all your wonder? You have no idea how much time you have on this planet, but you could discover who you are in it. So, let's work with what you've got, build on your foundation and set foot in the direction of your dreams.

Here's my story…

I was pushed out of the darkness in 1981. All nine pounds and four ounces of me (my poor, petite mom). I was her only child, but my dad had three children from a previous marriage. We lived in a big, new four bedroom home, so there was room for my half brothers and sister to visit on weekends.

My first memory of really being happy was when I was three years old, dancing on the fireplace hearth. My mom was video-taping my slick moves to *"On the Loose"* by SAGA while my dad stood beside me smiling. I made a cool spin maneuver and then pointed to my dad and said, "Now you." He broke into a twist.

I felt elation sweep over my body. Watching my dad break free with his old man groove lit my spirit up. I remember feeling so alive watching him and being in the pure love of it all. I got back to my dance as joy trickled through my body. As my mom witnessed us in our innocence and essence, it gave me a deep feeling of wholeness. A feeling my spirit craved and wanted to build upon.

Then one day not long after, I was being held by my Nana outside a big concrete building while my parents filed for divorce. Listening back to the lyrics of that song, maybe there was a new meaning. Just when we think life is one thing, it can quickly turn to another. That picture perfect family life I grew up watching on TV wasn't going to be mine. Mom and I moved into a low-income CO-OP housing community, and Dad left town.

My tickle trunk became my new happy place. Mom kept it stocked with fun masks, costumes, old high heels and rockin' eighties attire. Friends would come over and all I wanted to do was dress up and perform. I loved to lip-sync to Madonna, Tina Turner and Whitney Houston. Any time Mom had dinner guests, they were getting a show whether they wanted one or not. I loved putting on a show.

My Montessori teacher Ms. Linda remembers me as a very curious child. I'd rather browse around all the work stations to see what everyone else was doing instead of staying at my own. I absolutely had to move. Fascination got the better of me as I'd roam around until I found something of interest. When I did, I would get really excited about what I had discovered and summoned other kids over to take a look. As the crowd of scampering feet came over to take a peek at my findings, I would be off again to the next discovery. Ms. Linda had to work extra hard to keep her classroom under control when I was in it.

I tried piano, jazz, ballet, basketball and other sports, but I had a hard time committing to the rigidity and repetitiveness of it. I'd love it for a bit and then I'd need to break free and do my own thing.

Some said I had a short attention span. This is how I think of it: I always needed to do "ME" in my own way, feeling whatever I wanted to feel, doing whatever I wanted to do, even if it wasn't always good for me. My mom allowed this kind of behaviour, which I know is unusual. She encouraged me to try new things and feel my feelings. She provided a safe space for me to explore and expand.

At the time, Mom was going through her own self-exploration and had found a safe haven to express her feelings at a retreat centre a few hours away. They had just started a kids' program called *Kids in the Spotlight (KITS)*, so on one of her trips, she took me along.

Miss Denise, the program organizer, was very tapped into the little human psyche. Somehow, within a few days, she'd have a group of twenty-plus children from the age of three to eighteen putting on a theatrical performance, like CATS or Fiddler on the Roof.

I later found out the purpose of the performance was to receive peer to peer learning, something the school system doesn't facilitate but is in fact the optimal way for a young person to learn. As a kid in the program, I just remember admiring the kids who were older than me and wanting to be like them. I also felt good about who I was and what I brought to the table. It was a place for true expression in a safe and supportive environment. I was so young that I had no idea what the plays were about, but I loved being a part of something with people who truly saw me.

Here is a letter from Miss Denise that I've kept:

"Without energetic leaders such as yourself, we all get tired and beige. I think back in those days, girls were being repressed and when they had energy, they were labeled as bossy, told to settle down. So I want to add

*that learning, taking your space and being comfortable about it, doesn't have to cramp anyone else's style - that you make room for others while you lead and hold vision was something I saw you learning - yes even when you were wee, wearing leg warmers and glittery everything! I also remember dancing with you on a hot sunny day. We had all the doors and windows open to invite breezes and stay cool while we danced to very lyrical music that called for lots of big arm sweeps and slow battements. We were so free! Then you showed your Mom the dance you made up - her generous smile warms my heart. You always added a little swagger to every move, even though it didn't really need it. The move was fine without it, but it was your stamp. You and your mom were such a glamorous pair - your mom had lots of snake themed accessories that were quite sexy - and you had a sort of **fearless cockiness to you that was quite endearing**."*

When I got to elementary school, the school counsellor told me I had A.D.D. I hadn't ever heard of that before. She said it was the reason I had a hard time sitting still and doing what I was told.

Later in my life, I decided that A.D.D. stood for: Adventure, Determination and Desire. I wasn't ever interested in doing what everyone else was doing. I didn't care about following the crowd. In fact, sometimes I thought what the crowd was doing was dumb.

That "other voice" in my little head would look at the constructs of the world and say, "Why are we doing it this way? Why is everyone so serious around here? Aren't we supposed to be having fun, following our joy and being playful?" School, Dance, Parents, Teachers… they all acted so stuffy. Like everyone was in a boring choreography of their own life that they couldn't escape from. Adults looked sad and tired. It was like they would try to enjoy themselves but ended up sapping all the fun out of whatever they were doing to make it predictable or responsible (whatever that was). When I'd question people's methods, I would get into trouble.

They would shout things like, "Well, this is how it's done. This is the way it is!"

That didn't sit right with me. So, I tested it.

In Grade 6, our teachers went on strike. When they returned I thought, "Well, if the teachers can do it, we surely should be able to too." So, one day before class was about to start, I asked all the kids to come strike with me in the hall. Our teacher, Mr. Cousins, with coffee in one hand and paper in the other, came down the hall, only to be met by kids on either side of him yelling, "Strike! Strike! Strike!"

I piped up and said, "We're not coming to class."

He looked at us with a stern *"I'm not taking your shit"* glare and told us all to get to our seats or he would send us to the principal's office. Every kid except me hurried back into class. I wasn't afraid of the principal's office. I had been there many times before. In fact, I really liked our principal and his secretary. They were always really kind to me. It's like they knew I wasn't a bad kid, so they kept giving me the benefit of the doubt—which I abused. Still, they were right. I wasn't bad. Although I wasn't good either. I was just Adera, trying to find my way in the world. Teachers would tell me to "Listen," to stop being so "Disruptive," to "Sit Down," to "Do What I'm Told," but I didn't like doing things I didn't want to do. Things that didn't seem fun or interesting. And that voice in my head would again chirp up and say, "I don't know what you need to know this for! Why can't life be more like *Kids in the Spotlight?"*

Little by little, the world started to dim my light. Fitting in, comparison and judgement crept into my relationships with my classmates. I wondered why I couldn't be more like them. Why did I have to be so difficult and distracted all the time? How could all the other kids could sit still and I couldn't? Why wasn't I disciplined like everyone else?

On top of that, I developed a weird sense of body image. I seemed to be "bigger -boned" than the rest (that was how the adults put it). I also acted more grown up and looked older. It was like I was adult-ing in my eleven-year-old body quicker than the rest. What was wrong with me? I started taking advice and direction from people a few years older than me, trying to get an upper hand on where my body was taking me.

Mom and I had been living in my grandparents' attic so Mom could save her money for a nicer place. We had two single beds up there with a little sink and a closet for each of us. I remember grabbing the latch and hooking it into the ceiling, pulling down the folded staircase, and heading up the creaky wooden stairs, thinking, "none of my friends live in an attic." On nights my mom was out late, my Nana would cook dinner and I would rub her stinky feet while she watched *Wheel of Fortune*.

When my Dad eventually moved closer to us, I saw him on the weekends. When he picked me up, he wouldn't even get out of the car. We would speed off without saying goodbye to Mom. I thought we were so cool and reckless together. I loved being whisked away like that. With Dad, there were no rules, no structure, no school, no care. His signature phrase was, "Go play on the yellow line."

Sometimes we would go visit his parents, and my Italian grandma would make the most delicious pasta. We played cards while my uncles drank and smoked. Uncle Eddie told the best jokes and showed me the neatest card tricks. He felt like a rebel to me. I wondered if that side of the family was where my trouble-making streak came from.

On Sundays, my half brothers and sister would come over to Dad's house and we'd have a family dinner together. They were twelve, fourteen and sixteen years older than me so I tried desperately to fit into the conversation, but it never seemed to work. The minute I finally got a job, they talked about being in a relationship. The minute I got into a relationship, they got married, then had babies. I just couldn't keep up. Those are some of my loneliest memories.

Feeling completely unnoticed and questioning where I fit in, I would often ask myself:

Why am I here?

What is uniquely mine to share?

Why am I lonely?

Do I matter?

What is it that I am supposed to learn?

Then I had my first taste of love, and I had it all figured out.

Questions to Free Your Spirit

Throughout my Free Spirit journey, I could see that my younger self held a lot of clues as to who I wanted to be in the world. I do believe our little selves hold the keys to our purpose when we're able to ask ourselves questions about our stories.

1. The First Thing You Loved To Do

The experience of "putting on a show" has followed me throughout my career and life. I know now that it's part of my purpose.

So, I pose this question now to you: Can you remember something you loved to do when you were really small? Don't overthink it, just mentally note it. When you look back at old photos or videos, what activities or hobbies are you enjoying? When did you feel happy, playful, fully alive?

2. Being Seen

When Miss Denise told me that I had "a sort of fearless cockiness that was quite endearing," I knew she had fully seen me for who I was.

Do you have a childhood memory of being seen? Perhaps think of a time when you were taking part in one of your favourite activities and adults or peers would say, "well done." Can you remember a time when someone took in your spirit as they watched you wholeheartedly?

3. An "Other Voice"

Do you recall having an "other voice" in your head? Do you remember what it said to you when you were young? Did it question the things you experienced?

2

LOVE: THE GREATEST SUPERPOWER IN THE UNIVERSE

Love takes over your entire being with its force. It's the most transformative emotion on the planet, and can become your demise.

Adam became my everything. I'll never forget laying eyes on him in Mrs.Taylor's first grade class. That day, I was convinced we would be married and be together forever.

I hit the jackpot when somehow our moms got to talking, and his mom offered to babysit me after school for a few hours while mine finished work. I pined for his undivided attention, trying everything I could to work Love Magic on him in those few hours. He was kind, but it was clear that he wasn't that into me. He'd rather watch TV, play video games or do anything but play with me.

And then, one day, it was as if my Love Magic had started to work. My Mom finally saved up enough money, and we moved out of my grandparents' attic and into a ground floor suite two blocks away from Adam. *Are you kidding me?* Dreams were coming true. Maybe things were going to work out after all.

Since Mom left early for work, it was suggested that I walk down to Adam's house and catch a ride to school with him.

Adam, his mom, his little brother and me would pile into their truck. I'd be smooshed against Adam on the bench seat. Our legs would touch the whole ride to school and I would just stare at our side-by-side knee caps and feel the warmth of his leg next to mine. I was in heaven. On hot days, though, that truck would get smelly. Morning breath mixed with young boy pheromones equaled a musty scent you couldn't forget.

I got my first period just before my twelfth birthday, before any other girl in my grade, and it was so embarrassing. Mom sent me to school with the biggest fanny pack full of different sized maxi pads. I was afraid to use a tampon.

I don't know what stirred the boys in my class that day—maybe they could sense my embarrassment—but they thought it would be funny to take my fanny pack and have a peek inside. On our lunch break, they snatched it from me and ran around the school yard while I frantically yelled at them to give it back. Adam was playing along too as he was a part of the "boys club," but he also noticed I was seriously distressed.

I thought I was going to *die*.

If Adam saw what was in there, what would he think of me? He'd know I was a freak, that's for sure. I was already bigger than all the other girls and this now would mean I'd be completely unlovable. He would never fall for me.

The one place where I couldn't chase them was the boys' bathroom so off they stormed inside. Since I was no stranger to the principal's office, I debated going inside, but something stopped me. I surrendered and cried as the door closed, thinking that was it. I was finished. *That fucking fanny pack is about to ruin my life.*

Within a few minutes, the boys came out of the bathroom and threw the fanny pack back to me. One of them mumbled, "I don't know what the big deal is." It was almost like they didn't really understand what was inside. It just looked like a lot of plastic wraps.

Adam came out last and said, "I couldn't stop the guys from looking in there but I didn't look."

Oh, thank God. I was so relieved. I was touched that he respected my wishes. It was sweet. He was clearly my friend.

By the end of Grade six, Adam and I would hang out after school. He taught me how to skateboard, smoke cigarettes, drink alcohol, sneak out of my house late at night and steal. Those weren't my proudest moments, but I was in love. Mom started to really worry about me. She was catching me sneaking out, acting reckless and dishing up rude remarks. She felt she had to do something. My Jonathan Brandis and Andrew Keegan posters were shifting to Eddie Vedder and Kurt Cobain posters. Her daughter was starting to grow up and not in a good way.

Mom received an invitation to go to Tulum, Mexico on a personal development retreat. Since there would be some other kids going as well, she thought this would be the perfect opportunity to remove me from my destructive adolescent environment and surround me with some self-inquiring adults. I got to take a friend and, luckily for me, there just so happened to be three teenage boys to hang out with as well.

There was one in particular who caught my attention. He had shoulder-length curly hair, the most beautiful smile and a hippy vibe that I wanted to learn more about. The boys were sixteen and nineteen, so my girlfriend and I lied and said we were fourteen just so they'd think we were cool. *Please don't ask me any high school questions. I'm only twelve.*

During the days when the adults-only workshops ran, the five of us would make our own fun. One day, we rented a car and visited the town and the cenotes. Another day, the boys took off with some older girls they met at the beach and suntanned nude. I spied on them through the bushes nearby wishing I had the balls (no pun intended) to do what they were doing.

I knew I was losing the one I had crushed on, as he found more interesting things to do with the other girls he had met. I would listen to *Gordon* by the Barenaked Ladies on my Discman, listening and lying in bed, Brian Wilson style, trying to figure out what I could do to win his attention.

One morning at breakfast, he walked by me and whispered, "Grab your food, I'll meet you in your room."

OMG! My heart started to race. *What did he want... maybe a kiss?* Nerves rushed over me. *I don't think I am ready for whatever is about to happen.*

I got a couple pieces of fruit and corn tortillas in a daze and walked with utter excitement back to my cabana. Mom was already in her workshop, so the coast was clear. I entered the cabana by the ocean and saw him perched on the windowsill, his long curly hair picked up by the soft breeze. The early morning sun shone on his perfect skin as he looked over at me. My heart was pounding with anticipation as I approached him anticipating his kiss.

He told me his parents had mentioned they were going to put on a talent show on the last night of the retreat. One of the older gals had offered to teach him how to salsa dance, and he wondered if I wanted to be his partner. *WHAT?! UM, YES, PLEASE. ME, PLEASE.* It wasn't a kiss but it was close. Trying not to sound too excited, I said, "Sure, that would be fun."

"Ok, our first lesson is after lunch. See you at the beach to practice," he said, and he was off.

YES! I get to hang with him every day to practice salsa before we leave to go home. That's better than nothing.

We met with the teacher three or four times and practiced another three or four times until it was show time. It was my very own *Dirty Dancing* moment. There were a few sexy moves and he would hold me so close when we danced. I freaking loved every minute of it.

On show night, we were the last to perform. I was so nervous waiting throughout the show for our big moment. The Emcee called us up and the music started to play. We locked eyes and danced. It was hot, it was fast, it was amateur, but it was met with a standing ovation and whistles from the crowd. Everyone could see our chemistry. I was beaming from ear to ear.

I never did get that kiss, but I did get exactly what I wanted. His attention. He had picked me.

When I swaggered back to school with my sunkissed skin, I had a newfound confidence. I had just gotten attention from a sixteen-year-old, and you can bet your bottom dollar I was bragging about it all over the school yard. Was I trying to make Adam jealous? Obviously!

A few weeks later, one of the kids brought over his Ouija board and set it up in the covered basketball court near the pick-up area after school. Adam's mom was late, so we sat down in curiosity and played a quick round together.

Suddenly, the boy who brought the game said, "How old will Adam be when he has sex?" Our hands moved from one to three. *OMG, that's next year.* Then the boy asked, "And who will he have sex with?"

A-D-E-R-A…*What? Me!*

We both looked at each other like "Ah, yeah, right," but we'd felt it in our hands. Something was directing us to those letters. I was scared, but also thrilled. *Could this really come true? Only time will tell.*

And it did. In the summer of Grade Seven, going into high school, Adam and I made it official. We became a couple that most likely was going to get married, so our parents could just calm down with the emotional upset over us always being together.

I felt as if I had definitely cracked the code to the meaning of life. It was to meet someone like Adam. The questions I had about who I was, why I mattered and why I felt lonely and in pain were gone. I felt a sense that my guides or God or whatever totally had my back. They were allowing me to have this experience so early in my life. I had figured it all out. I had found my One.

And lo and behold, when we turned thirteen, it happened. We had sex for the very first time and it was everything I had hoped it would be. LOVE MAGIC indeed. We spent every day together, getting up to no good on most of them. Mom would leave me a $10 allowance every day during the summer, so Adam and I would go uptown to the liquor store. We got chummy with the local homeless man who would sit outside the store collecting change and made a deal that if he got us booze, we would give him cigarettes. We'd always get a mickey of Dark Lamb's rum.

Our little beach town came alive in the summer with many hippy, drug-addled, fun humans by the ocean. We got to know all of them. We spent our days lounging in the sun, doing drugs and watching our crazy world go by. Adam and I had everything we needed.

Some nights, he would fetch me around one a.m. We'd head down to the field near our place and cuddle under the stars and talk about the universe. There was so much I was curious about and we'd be out there for hours just taking it all in.

Life seemed to be working out just fine for me even though my mom was always so worried. Also, I didn't always love who I was around Adam or how he was around me—but we could change. *Isn't that what happens? You change each other?* We could do anything together.

By the end of that summer in 1994, things were starting to fall apart. Adam and I took a break. We ended up going to different schools, so our worlds were separated.

Honestly, I was excited to meet so many new people. I got lots of attention from the boys from all grades and had another new boyfriend within minutes. I wanted to hurt Adam for not being who I wanted him to be, and I was desperate to find our love again in someone else. I thought it was all that mattered, even more than my education. My grades suffered and I did questionable things just to get the attention I needed. I wanted to feel that Love Magic from someone who got me, wanted to be with me and could be who I wanted them to be. I went through a handful of boyfriends looking for that special something I seemed to have only found in Adam.

During that time in my life, acting in school plays became one of the more positive things I had going.

Mom had heard of an after-school clowning class and thought it would be an interesting endeavour to keep me out of trouble. I was intrigued, and felt it was a way to at least escape all the heartache. Plus, I was curious to learn more about my silly, playful, attention-seeking, funny, out-there, daring persona. That class was a deep dive into your inner child and learning what it was that they wanted. We did a lot of meditation and unearthed what that child wanted to say. That was to be the basis of our clown character (no wonder clowns are so sad).

Around the same time, Mom threw me a "coming of age" spiritual ceremony with twenty or so women. They all gifted me something meaningful and sacred to help me make my way through life, including a carved half moon. We held hands in a circle and looked in each other's eyes as we sang "Return To Innocence" by Enigma. It was deeply touching.

This little half-moon meant a lot to me. I cherished it, as it represented all the women who stood by me, ready to see me flourish into a beautiful, abundant woman. Those women believed in me, even though I couldn't believe in myself. So, I named my clown character "Moon Spirit." She wanted to be playful, curious, accepting, light-filled, fun and free!

Eventually, a kids' TV show got word of Moon Spirit and wanted to do a feature on me. They filmed me putting on my makeup, getting into character and hitting the streets to entertain boys and girls with my balloon characters and fun-loving attitude. I began to be booked for birthday parties and special events. I even surprised my boyfriend on his birthday in his twelfth grade English class with balloons, in full Moon Spirit makeup. He was mortified. Thinking back on it, I was crazy. That was crazy.

Being on stage and the centre of attention was always a thrill for me. It was a way to escape reality and the thinking mind. I couldn't zone out on lost love or I'd miss a step. It forced me to be in the present moment. Performing sparks such an intensely alive feeling. It can be a bit addicting, like a drug, except you get praise at the end of it, not judgment. I was definitely hooked. I loved it more than alcohol. I was thinking this could be my career. Acting…or even better, having my own TV show. It sounded pretty ideal to receive accolades, awards and recognition for just being myself.

So where do you sign up for that exactly? That was the thing: my world didn't seem to have the opportunities I was looking for. It didn't seem set up to support my big dreams. I was getting the sense that what I wanted didn't exist yet and I would have to be the one to create it. But I had no idea how to do that.

So, instead of creating something out of nothing, I hung with the misfits. It felt easier to dim my light than figure out how to BE ME in a world that so clearly didn't have a support network in place to allow it. I drank, smoked, did drugs and had sex. I was a lost teen.

Sometimes, I would try to be a "drama kid," a "sporty kid," or a "student council kid," but I would always feel like an outsider. I didn't know who I was. I wanted to keep exploring and experimenting. I loved to try new things. Drugs gave me a peek into worlds I didn't even know existed that seemed pretty awe-inspiring, thrilling and crazy fun, and my spirit craved that. My spirit simply wanted to know why it was here, and that was something I believed I would only find out with the misfits. I did, on occasion, have some epiphanies around how drugs and drinking were keeping me dull and would spend time exploring other alternatives, but nothing stuck. My misfit friend group was safe place. Even though we were nuts, I felt accepted. We would talk about life, our feelings, our experiences and would get up to some wild shit. Some of our antics were less than desirable and dangerous at times, but I felt so invincible then. Like my body would survive no matter what. Fear only dogged me when I was without a boyfriend or questioning what life was all about. When my friends and I were on drugs, drinking or smoking, we bonded over the magic of life, feeling limitless and free. I found it more entertaining than being a part of mediocrity.

When our school got a youth counsellor, I decided to test her out because she was cool. I decided to participate in the smoke-free camping trip she arranged. I journaled why I smoked and what it was like not fitting in at school. With my permission, she sent it to the local paper. They decided to do a full-page story about me and my experience. So, with the bread-crumb trail of my acting, clowning and journaling ahead of me, I convinced myself that maybe, just maybe, I could make a career of being myself.

When I had just barely graduated from high school, I moved from our small beach town to the big city in pursuit of my TV show star dreams. I had zero direction, but I was cocky. I thought with my experience I would easily get an agent, work in commercial and film, maybe go to broadcast school and bada boom, bada bing, have my own show. I figured all that would take two years tops. By the time I was twenty, everything I wanted would be mine, give or take.

At the time, I was still seeing a guy from high school who had knocked me up just a few months earlier. I'd decided to have an abortion because I was clearly not ready to be a mother. I was still striving so hard to belong and deeply addicted to finding love in another. I couldn't imagine being responsible for someone else, let alone a baby.

This was about the time that my underlying anxiety decided to kick into full gear, resulting in my first real panic attack. I woke up alone in the middle of the night sweating, unable to catch my breath and too afraid to go outside for air. I sat on my toilet with the window wide open trying to get oxygen into my lungs, wondering what the hell was happening to me. I had no control over my body while I shook, fear pumping through my veins.

Where am I? Who am I? Everything seemed so fucked up.

At least I still had my steady boyfriend. He surely would help me get through this. He was all I could think about, and I couldn't wait to see him.

I'd chosen to move into a ground-floor suite just a few blocks away from his work, hoping one day we'd move in together. But none of my plans worked out. When I asked him to come for dinner or stay the night, he preferred to drive fifty minutes to his home than stay with me.

I was starting to become that crazed girlfriend, dropping off lunch at his work, phoning or texting too often during the day and night, trying to get to the bottom of why he didn't want to be with me, especially while I was facing all this crazy panic. I was full of worry over what the future would bring. I needed him and it was all consuming.

Why doesn't he need me too?

I thought we were so good together. We rarely fought, we always had fun, we'd gone through an abortion together… so why didn't he want me?

Why did I keep falling for guys that were just not that into me? Over and *over* again? And when a guy really did like me, I was aloof. I really wanted the hard-to-get cool guys. Not the "you're a princess, I will do anything for you" kinda guys.

Despite my panic and relationship troubles, entering my twenties was still pretty amazing.

I had a job and a great group of actor friends. I was hanging out in the right comedy clubs and meeting the right people. I had my own car, and a new place with a roommate. I had been around the block a few times and felt pretty confident in what I was really looking for in a man. It was definitely Adam. So, I decided to move back to our beach town and move in with him and his parents. I got a job nearby and took charge. I painted his bedroom in army colours, sponging on dark green, brown and black. I thought it was brilliant (sorry to his Mom now). I was convinced that this time we would make this work.

I still ventured out to the city every other night for stand-up comedy or improv training. By month three, I thought, *I can't do this*. Adam could barely hold down a job and had none of the same ambitions or hobbies as me. He was really into heavy lifting and heavy metal and I was more into raving and rehearsing. Back when we were kids, we'd bonded over our hurt and our questions around life. Now I was in it, wanting to experience it. Wanting to live large and see where it took me and what big adventures I could get up to. Gradually, it became clear: Adam just wasn't coming with me.

One day when he was in his garage gym working out to loud heavy metal music, I got my best friend to pick me and my things up. Secretly, I'd found a roommate and an apartment back in the big city. I will never forget the look on Adam's face when he came out to the driveway as I pulled away. We didn't really even get a proper goodbye. I was too ashamed. We just looked at each other as if to say, *this is really over*.

That was the last time I saw him.

Questions to Free Your Spirit

Our choices create our results. Our feelings towards those choices dictate how we live and what our beliefs inevitably are. It's important we look back at mishaps and struggles with an open heart and mind around how we created the patterns in our life so we can choose to see our circumstances in a new light. It's also necessary to see where we derived meaning in our lives, what kinds of people or experiences made us feel accepted and how we may have already learned to detach our sense of self from external validation.

1. First Love

Do you remember your first love? What was it about them that you admired or adored? What turned you off about them? Who were you with this person?

2. Being Wanted

Have you ever asked yourself, "Why doesn't he/she want me?" Looking back now, what do you think the answer was?

3. Independence

When you finally had a taste of independence, did you feel lost or secure in your place in the world? What gave you a feeling of meaning? Was it your job? Your hobbies? Your relationships?

3

LET THE ADVENTURES BEGIN

I'M FREE. I'M YOUNG. I'M READY.

How do you know who you are if you don't have wildly uncomfortable experiences to show you?

City life offered so much. It was full of opportunities, people, and experiences. I seriously couldn't get enough! I wanted to try everything.

I thought one of the gals I worked with was pretty cute, and since I hadn't had much luck with men up until this point, I thought, W*hat the heck. I'll ask her out on a date. I wonder what it would be like to be "the guy" for once.*

I was intimidated by her. She was one of the assistant managers at the restaurant I worked at. We really didn't say much to each other even though every time I passed her, I would try and flirt by asking her a question or making a joke. She didn't really get the hint, so one day after my shift I mustered up my courage. I walked up to her with butterflies fluttering in every inch of my body and asked her blank, "Would you like to go out for dinner and see an improv show with me one day?"

She looked at me with her usual *I don't show emotion* bitch face, then cocked a smile and said, "Sure."

"Cool, would next Friday work for you?"

She said she'd check her schedule and get back to me. The next day, she gave me a nod during our work hours, letting me know that we were on.

I picked her up in my sporty, souped up '91 Civic and took her out on the town. The local comedy club was my regular hangout, so I was hoping to look like a celebrity upon arrival, but no one I knew was there yet. We got a table at the back, had dinner and then moved up to the bar for the show. Now my friends were starting to trickle in and I was feeling cool, introducing her to the performers for the evening. After the show, I drove her home and said, "Thanks for the lovely evening." She leaned in and I kissed her. I had practiced this in high school with my best girlfriend, so I knew I could do that part. Then she asked me if I wanted to come in for some fun. She definitely was giving me the sexy vibes. I got scared. I said I had to wake up early for my shift tomorrow, but really appreciated the offer. Maybe next time?

There was no next time. I just wasn't that into her.

I hate to admit it, but it felt good to be the jerk for once. I was on a roll. I was twenty-one and had been single for almost a year. I felt super in the groove with my life and what I was doing.

Stardom wasn't far now. I could feel it. I had just been accepted as the youngest resident in training at the city's biggest Theatre Sports League and had successfully pulled off my first stand-up comedy routine. I was in the swing of it, except I had also racked up my credit card to over $5,000 late night drinking at clubs, buying rounds, and acting like a big shot. It was my favourite thing to be. So, I had to sell my cool ass Civic and start taking the bus. Not cool.

One day, I was on the bus going to an audition, going over my lines. As I looked out the window, I noticed the good-looking bus driver going in the opposite direction on the same route. He caught my eye. He was young and buff by the looks of it. (Not common traits of bus drivers.) He wore a pair of red Terminator sunglasses. When I got off at my stop a few minutes down the road, I asked my bus driver if he knew who that guy was wearing those sunglasses going in the other direction about five minutes ago?

He said, "I think that's Scott."

"Oh, do you know if he's single?"

"I'm not positive but I think he might be."

Huh. Good intel. Thank you, Bus Driver Man, for giving a crazed twenty-one year-old those private details about your co-worker.

After my audition, I hopped back on the #17 and asked the bus driver, "How does this route work? Like, do you have this route all day? Is it a loop? What does your shift look like?"

He told me.

I rode that bus for probably another week until I spotted Scott. I clocked the time I passed him, then ran home to look at the route on a map, trying to figure out when he would be outside my house. *GOT IT.*

This was before social media. You did what you had to do.

The next day, I went out wearing a short skirt, long jacket, high-heeled boots and a mid-drift shirt. My twenty-something body was the bomb. It was sprinkling a little outside, so as he pulled up to the stop, I had my umbrella up, hiding my face, my heart beating hard. When he opened the front doors, I took a big breath in, then lowered the umbrella to reveal myself and smile. *Show time!* It was very well choreographed, if you ask me. Where were the cameras?

I walked up to him and said hello. As I showed him my bus pass, he gave me a friendly glance and nod. I headed to the back of the bus, thinking, *Oh god, what have I done? He's clearly not into me.*

Better up my game!

I got on my cell phone and talked as loud as I could to no one on the other end, hoping he'd fall in love with my laugh and boisterous voice.

It wasn't working.

I really had nowhere to go that day except ride his bus, so I had time to figure out another strategy.

About fifteen minutes in, the lady in the seat directly across from the driver got off the bus and I thought, *Now is my time. The coast is clear! I can just hop right up there and start a conversation with him. He's going to love me. Let's do this. It's now or never, Adera, GO, before some old lady sits in that seat!*

Up I got, trying to walk as gracefully as possible down the aisle. I gently slid into the seat and opened right away with: "So, Scott, tell me, what does it take to become a bus driver?"

Oh my God. Did I really not plan something better than this!?

He turned to me and said, "What did you just call me?"

With a look of *oh shit, this is bad*, I said, "Scott...that's your name, right?"

"How did you know my name?"

"Oh...aaahhhh...I was asking other bus drivers about you..."

Oh God, shoot me now.

He looked at me for a second and then started to laugh. *Oh phew.*

He's got a nice laugh. It felt like I was saved by being adorable. *Adera the Adorable. That's me.*

We chatted for about thirty minutes until he asked me what stop I wanted to get off at. *Oh right, geez.* I couldn't tell him I actually didn't have a destination besides meeting him. *Think, think, look around, where were we? Yaletown... who do I know around here? Oh, got it:* "Oh, I am going to go and check out the headshots I had done a few days ago. I'll get off at the next stop."

I quickly got out a pen and paper and wrote my number down and told him to call me if he was interested in going for a drink some time. He took off his sunglasses and looked at me with his deep, much-wiser-than-me, crystal blue eyes and said, "OK, I'll give you a call."

Oh, Lordy me, it worked! With a *trying to not look too eager* smile, I bounced in joy off the bus. As he drove away, I hopped, skipped and jumped down the sidewalk, unable to hide the shit-eating grin on my face. I had a deep sense of satisfaction trickle through my being. By risking my pride, and being ok to look the fool, an opportunity presented itself that otherwise wouldn't have come to fruition.

Two days went by and no sign of Scott. I must have checked my phone every other minute. It was a Friday night and I was laying on my bed, a bit sad that he hadn't called. I was debating what I was going to do next when all of a sudden, the phone rang.

"Hello?" I said.

"Helloooooooo," he said in a sexy yet playful voice. "This is Scott calling."

My heart skipped a beat. Acting coy and aloof, I said, "Oh, hi! How are you?"

"Good."

"So, are you taking me up on my offer for that drink?"

"I guess I am." He laughed.

We made plans to meet the next day to go for dinner at one of my favourite spots in the city.

I was nervous. I really knew nothing about this guy except for the fact that he had a good job and he supposedly was single and he had light blue wise eyes. *How old is he?*

As it turned out, ten years older than *me*! Scott had been separated for six months from his wife, a woman who had cheated on him with his best friend. *Ouch.* My parents were ten years apart so I thought, *it can't be that bad*, even though they hadn't worked out. It was still worth a try.

We didn't have a load in common. Our lifestyles were totally different. I loved to drink and go to live comedy and improv shows. He loved to go to martial arts class and listen to music from the seventies. I loved to hang out with my friends and go on adventures. He loved to go to his full-time job and be a boring adult.

Oh well, we can make this work, I thought. Even though Scott was hesitant and brought up all the reasons we shouldn't, I still pressed on. So, we moved in together and got a dog. That should keep me at home, I figured.

I played housewife for a good year. I gained twenty pounds and pretty much left the acting scene to hopefully build a life with straight and narrow good guy Scott.

We rented a really nice apartment twenty minutes from town and, well, it wasn't long before things really weren't working. I missed my old life, my friends, my ambition, my freaking *youth,* goddamnit. I was only twenty-three and had a lot of spunk in me still. This whole settling down thing with a good paying job and responsibilities really was slowly choking the lively Adera out. Scott, the good and wise older man that he was, recognized this, and said many a night: "Adera, you gotta go live. You gotta go see the world!"

It would infuriate me. I kept assuring him that this was what I wanted, but he knew better. So, one night I took his advice. Even though it felt so painful to leave, I felt the calling deep in my heart. I had to go.

He understood.

At the time, I was working for this rich young woman from the States. She'd married a wealthy Canadian, had two kids and moved into a mansion in the suburbs. Her husband worked all day and night and she was left at home with her two Filipino nannies and no friends except me. I became her personal assistant/paid bestie. They had a spare 1,000 square foot room on the left wing of the house, so I asked her if I could move in for a few months during my breakup. She said yes.

Those months were the best! I basically became her partner. Her husband paid for us to take her young daughters to Disneyland in a private jet. Then we visited Arizona on a gals' shopping weekend. We'd hang out in the city at the nicest restaurants for lunch after private fittings at luxury brand name stores.

It distracted me from my heartache of missing Scott. I slowly but surely was starting to rev back up to that fun, adventurous Adera I knew I really was inside.

One night, I was over at my friends' place having a pity party. They were this beautiful couple I had known for a few years who were always in support of my decisions. I was drinking wine, telling them all about how I would be single forever and never meet my one. Scott and I were officially over. I knew I couldn't go back to my old life in the city. And I most certainly couldn't work and live with this rich woman forever, since her husband was cheating on her and things were inevitably going to fall apart. I didn't know what to do, where to go, or who to be! I felt stuck and domesticated. I had lost touch of who I was and what I wanted.

This beautiful couple who I totally adored said, "Well, you remember how we met right?"

They had told me their love story a bunch of times as I was so fascinated to learn about how they had found each other. They were the perfect match. I loved hearing about their wild adventures together. It gave me hope. Of course, I knew how they had met: on a cruise ship they both were working on.

"So, why don't you go work there, Adera?" they said almost simultaneously.

I signed up. I was hired. And within six weeks, I was flying to Miami to start my job as entertainment staff on a cruise ship.

Oh my GOD, I have died and gone to freaking crazy heaven.

The ship had over 4,500 passengers and 1,500 crew and I was one of them. It was one of the biggest ships of its kind at the time. It was like Las Vegas on water. I had never been on a ship before and this was something to behold. There was even a street that ran down the centre of it with shops, a restaurant, wine bars and a pub.

Everyone in the entertainment department was young like me, and I made friends instantly. I'd never had the opportunity before to have such a diverse group of friends from all different countries.

There were seven of us on the team and I was the only Canadian. The rest of the group was from Turkey, China, Australia, USA, Jamaica and Brazil, which rotated often as everyone's six-month contracts overlapped. I seriously was loving this!

The entertainment staff were responsible for hosting dance and theme parties, activities around the ship, trivia, bingo, parades and so much more. I couldn't believe I was getting paid to have fun, act, and entertain! We would learn dance routines for the different theme nights, take the stage and talk on a microphone to sometimes 1000-plus people, escort the captain to his dinner party on formal nights and welcome guests when boarding and disembarking the ship. It was literally all my favourite things rolled into one, and I was making American *cash* every two weeks.

On port days, a group of us would get off the ship and go tour around the Caribbean islands. We'd take pics of ourselves chilling at 5-star resorts, drinking Coronas at the most beautiful beaches, snorkelling on catamaran tours, holding iguanas over bikini bods, and scuba diving off the coast of St. Thomas, and then post them on newly developed Facebook. I was living the life!

It was by far the best job I had ever had. In fact, I had already had at least fifteen of them and one failed entrepreneur attempt. I was contemplating doing this for life and forgoing the on-land stardom. *This is so easy*. You had built in celebrity status, especially if you were the actual Cruise Director.

People used to say I reminded them of Julie from *Love Boat*. At the time, I had never seen the show, so I would smile, thinking it was a compliment. I just recently watched an episode out of curiosity and discovered Julie was a real ditz and hardly worked.

I'm sure they meant her friendly attitude and warm smile, right? They better have.

A few months in, I was in the cafeteria after hours grabbing a quick bite. I was putting my dirty dishes in an overflowing dish pit when all of a sudden, a water tight door started to close slowly on top of the hundreds of dishes. I panicked. I didn't know what to do, and I was the only one in there. How was I going to clear all these dishes out of the way in time? Impossible. And I saw no sign of a CANCEL button.

I started yelling for someone to stop it, but it was too late. Dishes started breaking in half. Porcelain was flying everywhere and I was in the line of fire, screaming, covering my face and thinking I had to get the hell outta there.

Within seconds, someone in the enormous dish pit heard the commotion and stopped the guard from closing. *Oh, thank God.*

Then, this random guy eating in the cafeteria had heard me, so he came running to the rescue to make sure I was OK. Our eyes locked.

I said, "Thank you. Sorry about that. I don't know what happened there. All of a sudden, this thing started to close and dishes were flying everywhere but I'm OK. I'm new. My name is Adera."

"No problem," he said. "I'm glad you're ok. My name is Federico."

Oh, Federico!!! Are you kidding me!? Shit.

After that mishap, he walked me back to my cabin. We got to talking and, well, I fell in love again.

Federico and I were together off and on for a couple of years. We were lucky to get the same contracts and be on the same ship, but when we went our separate ways for our three-month vacation, it was really hard. He lived in a one-bedroom home with his mom and grandma in Uruguay. I wanted so badly for him to come to Canada and be with me. But it wasn't that easy. I went to visit him and his family on one vacation and we tried our best to stay connected with long distance phone calls. Texting and FaceTime wasn't a thing then. I racked up $8,000 in phone bills!

Why *me* with the $8,000 bill and not *him*? It's because I was the one who was obsessing, of course.

We would constantly fight.

Fed didn't appreciate how flamboyant and fun I was, and he would always accuse me of liking somebody or doing this or that with other guys. All of which wasn't true. It started to really get to me, and I would start to question him too. I was convinced he was up to no good with other girls. It was intense and made me feel like I always had to be on my toes. There was zero trust and it made us both crazy.

Oh, but the lovemaking! It was really hot. The passion just fueled the fire.

I wanted Fed to know that I was legit, that I really wanted to be with him, so I bought myself a promise ring (yeah, you read that right). I told him that one day we would get married.

Oh, dear Adera. You are something.

Every time we said goodbye, we acted like it would be our last time seeing each other. It was such an emotional roller coaster, with the accusations, the heated lovemaking and the physical distance between us. He made no real attempts to move or travel to Canada and I couldn't see myself living in Uruguay.

My manager on the ship knew of our fights. I would show up to Emcee and be flustered. The work would always turn me around, but the minute I was done I would go back to the fight, always looking for a resolution. Each day the cycle would continue over something. Some guy, some girl, or some accusations. So mid-contract, the higher-ups transferred Fed to a different ship.

You'd think my heart would have been relieved that this mayhem had ended, but no. I fought tooth and nail to get him back. I felt so sorry for myself and I was distraught that we couldn't be together. We loved each other soooooo much, and I had a ring to prove it.

Oh, dear Adera. You *are* something.

One day, our ship arrived into port with his. We had been apart for a few months now and I was elated to finally see him in Cozumel.

Once we docked, I was the first off the ship. I boarded his ship and went on a mission looking for him. They said he was working, so I went to where he would be, but he wasn't there.

I went to his cabin, where his roommate said he hadn't come back that night and wasn't there. Someone said he was in the storage room getting something. He wasn't there. *What the hell is going on? He knows he is seeing me today. Why can't I find him?*

I went back to his cabin, my heart pounding. I had the distinct impression that he was with someone else. As I was coming down the hall, I had a glimpse of him bolting into his cabin. I waited a couple minutes, then knocked on the door.

He opened it with his shirt off and hair a bit messy like he'd just woke up.

"Hey," I said, "where were you? I've been looking all over for you!"

"I've been here," he said, "sleeping."

"No, you haven't. I came here an hour ago and your roommate said you didn't come home last night."

"I guess he didn't see me, but I was in my bed."

Mmmm, ohhh kaaaaay. This was some serious bullshit. I told him to get dressed and meet me upstairs in the lounge. We needed to talk.

He arrived twenty minutes later and I prepared myself for "the talk." My heart was officially broken.

I wasn't completely surprised. He did to me exactly what he had done to the girl before me. When I met him, he was still in a relationship with another gal from another ship. He'd always said she wasn't coming back to ships, so he knew it wasn't going to last long. He left her hanging with daily phone calls for months while we were together.

I told him I couldn't do this any longer. I told him how fucked up life had been since we'd been together and how I wanted nothing to do with the fights, the lies, the long-distance, the constant state of worry and mistrust. It was eating me alive inside, and being without him was so painful and lonely. I just couldn't do it anymore.

He could hear my pain, which was surprising, and knew I was probably right. We both still didn't want to let go fully. He promised to do better and if my memory serves me correctly, I think we solidified our break up with one last passionate love-making session.

It was the closure I needed.

I remember the final goodbye on the docks of Cozumel. Hugging, kissing, holding hands, and promising that it wasn't the end—but it was.

It broke me in two, and I swore men off for years. It was going to take me a while to recover from this intense, abusive, physically, emotionally and financially draining relationship.

Questions to Free Your Spirit

1. Experiments

Have you experimented with your sexuality? What did you learn about yourself?

2. Doing What Doesn't Feel Right

a. Have you been in a relationship with someone who you knew wasn't right for you but you stayed anyway? Why did you stay?

b. Have you been in a relationship that lacked trust or respect? How did that make you feel?

c. Did you ever do anything crazy (like my $8,000 phone bill) to keep your relationship alive and going? Did you jeopardize your job or loss friends for love?

d. Have you been cheated on? If so, how did that make your spirit feel? Of if you were the cheating one, how did it feel to do that to someone else?

3. Make A List

Write out in point form a list of things you are engaged with at this very moment that don't feel 100% right to your heart.

EXAMPLE:

- Eating too much
- Not being as active as I'd like
- Not being as patient with my kids
- Stressing about work
- Not being honest with my Mom

It could be little things that maybe you spend a lot of time thinking about yet are shaping your reality. To free your spirit means to be completely truthful about who you are and clear with what you want. Remember that this exercise is meant to help you just notice your tendencies, not berate yourself in any way.

When I look back on my relationship with Fed, I can see how I too played into our destructive pattern. I engaged in things that didn't feel right to my heart, but ignored it due to my need or desire to be wanted.

4

LEANING INTO MYSELF

BECOMING WHO I REALLY AM.

Finding your truest expression takes guts. It can be perceived as socially unacceptable for most as the majority haven't taken the time to explore it for themselves.

Fed really took it out of me. My faith in men had been annihilated by that emotional atomic bomb. I didn't think I would ever be able to date again.

I needed a real break. I had been in and out of (what I thought) were very serious relationships since I was thirteen and I needed to regroup and figure out what the hell I was doing wrong. I knew it was going to be a while before I could be into another guy. I didn't want to give up on love, but I just didn't have anything left to give.

I had to choose whether cruise ships were going to be a life-long career or a thing I just did for shits and giggles. I decided on the latter and moved back to the city. Soon, I landed a dream job at a big local radio station as a promo girl. My job was going out to events on weekends, driving the company car and getting invited to all the big industry parties, launches and grand opening events. I even had backstage passes to pretty much any concert that came to town. I met Michael Bublé, the Barenaked Ladies, and Josh Grobin. Plus, I had floor tickets to performers like Beyonce and Nickelback.

I found my own little cute patio place. Literally, it was the front patio of a character house that had been converted into a 300 square foot suite with a bathroom. It was just a bit bigger than my crew quarters on the ship, so I thought, *Heck yeah, let's do this! Let's follow that dream. Oh yeah, what was it again?*

The acting thing had come and gone. Now I was more interested in being a talk show host, or maybe a radio show host. I had easy access to all the producers and hosts in town as our station was linked to a big media conglomerate.

Now that I'm totally in with the who's who of media this literally should take no time at all. I had become the chosen sidekick to a well-established producer in town, and had tickets to all the cool media-only parties. I met players in the industry daily. I thought for sure that within a year I would be the next morning show host or better yet have my own syndicated tv show, like Oprah!

Things couldn't be better. I was solidly single, mending my beautiful heart and keeping my word to myself that I wouldn't jump back into the dating scene too quickly. Yet I was meeting so many cool people at the same time. I could feel my career starting to take shape.

By the time I was with the radio station for about seven months, I'd had numerous cracks on the air doing in-house commercial spots. One of the DJs gave me access to her recording studio on weekends to try out talking to myself, which I didn't really dig. It felt weird going on and on, like I was having some riveting conversation with the airwaves, hoping that someone was listening. I knew I wasn't cut out for radio. I was too social and didn't like sitting by myself in a dark room being entertaining. Even if I had a host to bounce off of, radio wasn't really how I envisioned fame.

At Christmas, the company put on a huge party at a swanky hotel in town for our station and three others we owned in the area. The grand prize of the evening was a trip for two to Jamaica courtesy of one of the clients we mentioned every hour on the radio. To play to win, we had to get in a huge circle on the dance floor and turn our backs to each other. The Emcee called heads or tails as he flipped a coin in the air and we were to decide before he called it out loud whether we picked heads or tails by either placing our hands on our ass or head. There were a hundred or so participants at first, but we eventually got down to two: the main morning show honcho who I had met briefly, and me. We stood back to back and up the coin went. I had a few drinks so I was just winging it with little to no care. I had my hands confidently placed on my head when the Emcee asked if we'd made our final decision. I don't know what came over me but I quickly switched to ass and then nodded my head.

"TAILS!" the Emcee yelled.

I swung around to look at the morning show man, and he had his hands on his *head*.

OMG, OMG, did I (the new kid on the block) just win two tickets for an all-inclusive trip to Jamaica?

I sure had. Everyone came over to congratulate me while I smiled in total shock. I had won this unreal romantic $6,000 plus holiday and I had no man to spoil. *Fuck me.*

Who the hell am I going to take...?

The character house I lived in had four other suites. I had gotten to know Holly, the single girl my age who lived on the main level, really well. She had just moved for work from back east and didn't have many friends on the west coast. Almost every night before bed we would sit out on the covered porch and smoke cigarettes with a night-cap of my dad's questionable home-made wine (which was free so I never complained).

Holly became my BFF in a flash. She knew of all my heartbreak, all my newfound success and all my desires to meet someone who was right for me. We would talk about our dream men some nights into the wee hours. She was also recovering from a bad breakup. We kept each other sane by comforting and confronting one another when we were debating bad choices like calling or messaging exes.

We had gone on a girls' trip that summer to wine country and had had a wonderful time together, so I knew she'd be a great travel companion. I was so excited to tell her the news and invite her to come with me to Jamaica.

The next night after my big win, we were on the patio all bundled up with blankets and candlelight. We were finishing our first smoke and half-way through our wine when I said, "Hey, I have a question for you."

"K."

"What would you say if I offered you an all-inclusive trip to Jamaica for seven nights?"

"Whaaat?" She said with a smile on her face, her nose ring catching the light of the candle on our porch table. "What do you mean, trip to Jamaica?"

"Have you been before?"

"No. I haven't been anywhere!"

"What, really?" I had been to Jamaica a handful of times already with the cruise ship. *Oh well, this solidifies my decision even more. She is so deserving.* "Well, remember the company Christmas Party last night? They gave away a trip to Jamaica, and I won it!"

"Oh my God! No way!"

"And I'd like to take you as my plus one!"

Holly's eyes were wide with shock and excitement, trying to digest the information. I started to tear up.

"Are you sure you want to take me? I mean, you could take anyone!"

"You're right, but I want to take you!"

Holly started to cry too.

"So, is that a yes?"

"Yes! I would be honoured to go!"

Alrighty then. Let the single twenty-seven year-old gal trip to a five-star resort commence.

This was going to be fun!

As soon as Holly and I could get a week's vacation we were off. The minute we stepped onto the resort grounds, we were treated like royalty. This was probably the nicest hotel I had ever stayed at, with food, drink, tours, watersports and spa *all* included! The grounds were immaculate, and the beach was white sand with hotels lining it for miles in one direction and a rocky alcove in the other. It was, of course, a gated community, which meant there was nothing authentically Jamaican about it. I was disappointing about that. I had seen my fair share of segregation over my travels and it was always disheartening to witness.

The first day, we dropped our luggage off in our room, put our swim suits on, grabbed two rum punches and hit the beach! After an hour of suntanning, I thought, *What the heck; I'm gonna give wind surfing a try. Why not?*

I went to the water sports desk and an instructor happened to be free to show me the ropes. After about fifteen minutes, I thought I was really getting the hang of it so the instructor left me to have a crack at it by myself. Confident me, I thought I would be fine to venture out a bit. But then the wind picked up and caught my sail. It started pulling me further and further away from the resort. I started to panic and made some crazy amateur maneuvers to get closer to shore, but everything I did only took me further away. I was headed towards the jagged rocky shore, doing my best to get around it and to the sandy bit. I had no idea where I was. I was so disoriented and exhausted by the time I could touch the ocean floor.

Safely ashore, I looked up in relief and saw a sea of penises. I had landed on a private gay nude beach filled with old men.

Awesome.

I apologized profusely as I made my way back to sea to try and figure out how the hell I was going to get around the breaker and back to my beach. I dropped my sail, laid on my board and paddled back with all my might to where Holly was napping in her comfy beach recliner.

When I finally pulled myself to shore with the heavy windsail in tow, Holly looked at me and said, "Wow, you were gone for quite a while. You must have really enjoyed yourself."

"Yeah…not quite…funny story."

She pissed herself when I told her what had happened and felt super bad that she hadn't known to come and help me.

I never did try wind-surfing again.

Instead, we spent quality time drinking punch by the pool and reading books. The book I decided to devour had just come out and was one of Oprah's favourites. It was called *A New Earth* by Eckhart Tolle, and I was mesmerized. Holly had to listen to me talk about it after every page! It must have been beyond annoying to be taken away from her novel to hear me work through my ego and pain body and start to piece together why all my relationships had gone south because of them. But my mind was being blown. *How could I not know this stuff? How did Eckhart get right to the core of my Truth?*

My eyes were opening up to my unconscious habits and patterns. I started to see the world differently from that very moment. I couldn't comprehend how it was happening, I just felt like something was starting to shift. I was becoming *aware.*

Of course, I wasn't going to get all spiritual on the trip and say no to the all-inclusive everything. But I was excited to turn a new leaf when we got home. I decided to eat right, not drink and smoke so much and clear my head.

It was a thought anyway…Habits do die hard.

When we returned home, I had a new lease on life. I went to the local spiritual book store and bought some more eye opening reads by authors like Deepak Chopra, Louise L. Hay, Wayne Dyer and Don Miguel Ruiz. I started to get to work.

Right away, my inner work had me in a bit of conflict with my party lifestyle because I didn't know how I would give up that part of my identity.

One afternoon at work, I was out at a winery for a sponsored radio event and I saw a band make their way to a cute little wooden planked make-shift stage and introduce themselves as the "North Country Gentlemen".

The lead singer had a three-inch red bandana wrapped around his head with his shoulder-length long dark hair tied in an elastic band at the base of his neck. He was cute. They all were, but I always had a thing for the leads. The band started playing, and they were really good. The songs were fun, catchy and deep. They all sounded fantastic! I looked around to see if the smattering of people there were enjoying them as much as me. I really thought they had it all: the look, the talent, the sound.

OMG, Adera, where are you going with this?

After their performance, while they were packing up, I introduced myself and asked if they had a manager. They looked at me like *who is this girl, and no we don't.*

"Well, if you would consider it," I said, "I would love to represent you."

I told them I worked for the radio station and was sure I could get them on the air. They were flattered by my excitement and willingness. They pretty much on the spot said "What the heck? If this young, vibrant, enthusiastic woman thinks we have a chance and she has connections, let's do it!"

So off I went, creating posters, trying to nail down some gigs and getting everyone I knew at the record companies to listen to their track. I slipped their CD into the hands of every DJ at the station. I was in love with their sound. I also had a serious infatuation with the single lead singer and this was one way I was guaranteed to be around him. I got them a photoshoot, and booked them a few gigs.

Then my boss got word that I was sending their info and music to our contacts at the record labels.

Without warning, I was fired from my job.

Just like that. My actions constituted a conflict of interest. I was soliciting their music and abusing my power.

Holy Shit, what?

No!

No. NO. No. It was my dream job. Had I actually let my emotions for another guy ruin me again? Fuck me. And this one didn't even like me! Ugh. Shit.

I had to break it to the band that I had to quit. I had lost my job and our partnership wasn't working out.

They agreed.

What am I going to do now? Have I just destroyed my name?

I mean, everyone had to know what I did. They had to think I was untrustworthy and unethical.

OMG, what have I done?

My girlfriend, who worked for the local TV station, felt sorry for me and hired me to Emcee some movie premieres in the hopes that it might cheer me up. I was in a total funk. I didn't know what my next move was going to be.

One night after making my trying-to-sound-enthused "enjoy the show" type comments, I decided to do something other than go home and cry myself to sleep or finish off a bottle of Dad's home-made hooch with Holly. Instead, I figured I'd stay and watch the movie. It was *P.S. I Love You*, starring Gerard Butler and Hilary Swank.

Oh. My. God.

Was it ever the show for me! I cried, I laughed, I applauded. It couldn't feel more right. I felt it was a sign of what it was I was meant to do next.

I was in awe of Gerard's character. I couldn't believe how much he adored Hilary, and how much he wanted the absolute best for her and for her to go live her dreams more than anything in the world.

Man, I need me a guy like that! A man who sees me, gets me, and wants me to live my big adventurous, spontaneous life! Yes!

On my way home from the movie, I told Holly to meet me outside ASAP because I had some news. She reluctantly came outside for a quick nightcap even though it was 10:30 p.m. and she needed to be up early for work. She knew how fragile I was, and she was somewhat intrigued to hear the news.

"What's up?" she said, as she lit a smoke and cozied into her outside chair.

"This is it! This is what I've been waiting for, Holly! I am moving to Ireland to meet my man!"

She looked at me like, *Oh, god, here she goes. Because Ireland is where men like Gerard Butler live, obviously.*

I figured I'd been shunned in the city, and couldn't bear to show my face anywhere, so I might as well leave and see what I could make of myself in a foreign land.

This is the plan. This is it.

Holly was dumbfounded.

It took me ten days to get a one-year working Visa for Ireland, sell or store all my stuff, get out of my rental suite, pack my backpack and buy a one-way ticket to Dublin. All with only $900 to my name. I was embarking on my own *Eat. Pray. Love.* journey. I could feel it, and I knew I needed it.

Questions to Free Your Spirit

There were many clues into my true nature and what it was I wanted out of my life. Adventure. Determination. Desire (A.D.D) were key factors, along with experiencing many different avenues of interest. I had an ability to just go for something I wanted that I cultivated over the years so it was easier to say YES to possibility and to be able to creatively see an opportunity when it presented itself.

Dream Job

1. Did you ever land a dream job? What about the job was dreamy?

Blowing It

2. Have you ever gotten something that you really, really wanted and then blew it? How did you blow it? And why?

Crazy Ideas

3. Have you ever had a crazy idea like leaving the country or managing a band and you actually followed through? Did you get anything out of this choice?

Confidant

4. Have you ever had a friend you could tell anything to? Do you remember how it felt to have that kind of trusting relationship?

Stunts

5. Have you ever done something really stupid to impress someone? How did that turn out?

IRELAND

FINDING MY ONE TRUE LOVE.

Everything I ever needed. Everything I ever desired. Everything that's anything was there.

I couldn't have been in Dublin for more than an hour before ordering my first Guinness. I remember it tasted different—creamier, heavier, smoother than the brew we'd get back in Canada. They also served it closer to room temperature and never messed up the pour. I'd found a hostel smack dab in the middle of the city next to the O'Connell Street Bridge facing the River Liffey. The Guinness brewery was a twenty-minute walk down the road, so I was at the epicenter of authenticity. Pints were seven euros each, which was like $11 Canadian at the time. *At this rate, I'll be broke in a few weeks if I keep this up.*

Now, do keep in mind that I had done *zero* planning for this trip.

I shared a room in a hostel with six other girls for 40 euros a night so I knew I would at least be ok for a week. I had just enough time to find my bearings, get a job and a place to live. The resource centre with free computers, pamphlets and telephones was across the street, so that was a total saving grace.

But I couldn't forget that I had come to Ireland for a very specific reason. *To find my one true love*. I was not leaving the country until I had him, and that was that. I had my man radar turned onto high alert.

The first night in the communal kitchen, while all the foreigners made their Mr. Noodles and microwaved meals, I noticed one of the gals looking a little sad. She was clearly trying to hold back tears, sitting by herself. I went over and introduced myself. Her name was Linda and she was from Ontario. She had just arrived to Dublin the day before when she got some shocking news that her best friend had cancer. She was debating packing up and heading home to be there for her.

I could tell Linda was so sweet, kind and generous. We chatted into the night, bonding over cigarettes, Guinness (she introduced me to a place that served them for a reasonable price) and Canada. She had come to Ireland to live it up. She hadn't been anywhere really and thought she'd rock her independence and go live in another country for a year. We spent the next couple of days together, getting to know each other pretty well. When Linda decided to stick it out for a bit after her best friend back home told her to stay, I asked her if she wanted to find a place with me.

She loved the idea.

We found a newly renovated townhouse that had four bedrooms. We planned to share the downstairs master bedroom and ensuite. Of course, there were three other people we didn't know who lived there too. But we would only be sharing the laundry and kitchen with them so it was no big deal. We got the place for the going rate of 900 euros a month.

After putting in our security deposit and signing a six-month lease we frantically looked for work. Within the week Linda and I had both landed retail jobs at a clothing store on Grafton Street. We both made about 1,000 euros a month. After rent, the rest went strictly to partying.

Linda had heard my *P.S. I Love You* story and she was keen to accompany me on my man hunting adventures. There is an Irish pub called Whelan's in the movie, in the scene where Hilary and Gerard meet for the first time. I had to go! Maybe my Gerard would be there too. Could you imagine? I could! It was all I could think about. It was just a few blocks from where we worked, so after our shift around 9:30 p.m. we walked over for a pint. It was just like the movies. Loud Irish music, smoky, cramped, old and smelly… but no sign of Gerard. By this point I was starting to get a bit discouraged. All the Irish boys in the pubs seemed to love to wear matching track suits, drink way too much and practice questionable dental hygiene.

Not at all what the movie portrayed.

I didn't love it at the clothing store. Being on my feet all day, rehanging and rearranging clothes, dusting and being treated like an outsider by the fake nail wearing, glittery girls wasn't who I was. So, I worked hard looking for something more suitable, maybe something in travel or radio. After two interviews and a month of waiting, I finally got word that I had landed a job as a new sales rep for the biggest travel company in Dublin, selling cruises and trips to Florida.

These were things I was very familiar with. I was ecstatic.

Within weeks, I was one of the top sales people at the desk due to my Canadian accent and depth of knowledge. I loved the group of gals working there. They appreciated me, both for my experience and my personality.

One night after our shift a few of the gals invited me for a pint after work, curious to know what had brought me to Ireland. This was the first time I'd really hung out with the locals. I'd come to realize that when you're a foreigner you usually attract other foreigners.

So, I told them the truth about the movie.

They all looked at me a little dumbfounded. One gal piped up in her lilting Irish accent: "Oh, love, Irish guys are *nothin'* like that. Besides, Gerard is from Scotland."

What? No. What?

So, what you're telling me is I had the wrong country? FUUUUCCK.

It took me a few minutes to process this information. I could finally see why I wasn't finding any Gerards.

Motherfucker!

Research, Adera, research. It's a thing you know

I played it cool and tried not to look devastated and said, "It's all good. I'm just so happy to be traveling. I really love it here!"

Lies. I came for LOVE, for FUCK'S SAKES. I know in my heart that this time, it will be different. That this trip is going to be MY TRUE LOVE STORY. For real.

Ugh, god fucking dammit shit.

At my new travel job, I made more money, so I said to Linda, "Let's go! You came for adventure and travel so let's do it! I'll pay for whatever you can't."

So, we took a week off and flew into Germany. We rented a car and travelled all over, all the way to Austria and the Czech Republic. It was so awesome to see the sights with a fun friend.

Literally within an hour or so of flying, you could be in Paris, Edinburgh, London or Amsterdam, so on weekends when we had the money, we'd do just that! See it all! We travelled all across Ireland too, visiting castles, sacred monuments and natural wonders. I was secretly praying a Donegal lad would find me in Galway and that I would be his girl ("Galway Girl" is, of course, a song in *P.S. I Love You*).

Linda truly was a God-send. She was not only a super fun travel buddy, but on work days, if she got home first, she would make us both dinner. On nights when we both didn't feel like going out on the town, we'd stay in and eat chocolate covered digestive cookies dunked in tea and watch bad Irish shows on their local station RTÉ. She became my partner. I was so grateful to have her, even though we both knew our time would come to an end one day.

Sometimes you just need to curl up with a good girlfriend, a good flick and a good treat and the world seems to be a-ok.

I had been in Ireland for almost four months with no sign of my one true love. One night, walking home, I wandered through the side streets feeling tired and hopeless. Normally when I walked home instead of taking the bus, I would look to see if I had missed a place, a pub or a restaurant where he might be… but this time I was seriously questioning why the hell I was still in Ireland.

Did you really come all this way because of a movie?

Seriously, Adera?

You're an idiot.

You know, all the awesome self-talk that we're really good at when we make a mistake.

As I butted out my cigarette, I looked up and saw a sign in the window next to me that read, "Free meditation classes".

Well, since it was free, I thought, *What the hell, I'll check it out and see what they have to offer. I need something to cheer me up.*

I walked in and registered for class the following day.

The meditation group was like *nothing* I had ever experienced before. They all wore white. They didn't drink booze, smoke, drink coffee, eat meat or have sex.

WTF. This isn't good. How am I going to meet my love or have any fun without those things?

They were disciples of the Guru Sri Chinmoy. A few of the group's senior leaders had met him in New York and talked highly of their profound experiences in his presence. They said he was Godly. That he for sure was the real deal.

I had to see for myself. During the first meditation session, we watched a quick video on the master, to get into his vibration. Then they lit a candle and we stared at its flame for thirty minutes.

I was intrigued by these "followers" and their dedication to this way of life. My soul was craving solace. And it had been a while since I'd cleaned up my act with a drinking/smoking break.

I started attending meditations two to three times a week. I went off meat and fish. I quit smoking. I cut my alcohol consumption down to rarely participating, which was super annoying to Linda because we were party buds. Finally, I read all of Sri Chinmoy's books and started to meditate for an hour a day.

Guess what, Mom? I moved to Ireland and joined a cult.

Sri Chinmoy seemed like a wonderful man, a legit spiritual leader. He was all for world peace and unity. He expressed himself through his art, books and poems and had a supreme love for sport. He felt like an enlightened grandpa to me, leading me towards the light of a new way of life. Obviously, some of the rituals were a bit much— like staring at a picture of the Guru for hours at a time. I did, however, enjoy the group's yoga sessions and weekly hikes out in nature. It was important we exercised and challenged our body through physical fitness.

I quickly became a no-fun nun to Linda and the two of us started to drift apart. I was preaching self-awareness, self-study, self-liberation and the supreme consciousness. I was intense. I was in it to win it and literally all Linda wanted was to have fun, like we used to do.

Instead, I was starting to uncover parts of myself that had long been dormant in my being. Who knew that staring at a flicker of a candle for hours could turn a life around? I had reconnected with that curious child within and was starting to really question my purpose and true meaning again. I could see that since I'd arrived in Dublin, I'd been punishing myself with all this "carefree fun." Going out to bars, enjoying the night life, smoking and drinking too much, working at a temporary job just to pay bills and travel. I just stopped listening to my inner voice that was telling me to clean up my act and make more meaningful choices. And why? For losing the radio job. For being hurt so many times by men.

I had lost a sense of purpose. And it wasn't until I met my Sri Chinmoy family that I had a place to fully discover who I was again.

Linda's and my six-month lease was up, so I moved to a single room with a shared bathroom in a house on the other side of town.

Linda went home to Canada. Our parting was difficult, emotional. We had shared many amazing months together but I'd changed and we no longer fit together. It was hard to reconcile our friendship in a short goodbye, feeling like strangers as we considered how we would never see or be with each other again.

I was now completely alone on this journey. Even though I grieved the absence of my friend, I was curious to see where this next phase would take me. And how it would change me.

Walking to and from work took a silent hour each way. Some days after work, I'd stop at a public garden. I'd sit amongst the flowers for hours, taking in their beauty, watching the bugs do their thing —all while tapping into the deeper parts of myself with true joy. I loved contemplating my thoughts and listening to the world around me in this way. It was like I had blinders on and all of a sudden, I could see and hear everything. My long meditations and commitment to clean foods and behaviours had started to cultivate real mindfulness in me. This new lifestyle was the perfect breeding ground for my true feelings to emerge. I was in a space where I could honour and console them on my own. I didn't need someone else to complete me. It was the first time in my life I'd ever felt that way.

For three months I became my own life partner. I'd pray, meditate and write. I started to get really comfortable with being on my own. Suddenly, I was the gal walking down the street and smiling for no reason. My inner voice would say, *How cool is this? You're not smoking or drinking and you're having a ball. Just look at you strutting your life force.* I was in love with everything! I even took myself out on dates to fancy vegetarian restaurants. I wouldn't even bring a book. I went full Eckart Tolle, becoming completely content as a loner. I wanted to tell the world about my realizations, but I didn't.

Instead, I would write down my big visions and dreams in my trusty journal, holding space for my evolved self to take the stage one day.

On my days off work, I would hop on a bus or a plane and take myself on some adventure to a place I didn't even bother researching (not surprised?). I'd tour a new city just to be in its presence and honour its history. I lay in the grass along the waterway in Bruges, staring up at the clouds, fully embracing peace for the first time in my life. I was in awe of it all. I was embracing the energy that I was generating from within.

I decided to test my new found peace by booking a *singles* bus trip to Scotland to visit good ol' Nessie, the Loch Ness Monster. At the lake, I completely dropped the need to meet someone. I was finally content being with *me.*

I had met my one true love.

Myself.

Questions to Free Your Spirit

Self-love habits were the foundation for my new perspective on life. First and foremost, the relationship with yourself is the one that needs to be nurtured the most. When that happens, all other relationships, your work, a potential partner, your friends, your lifestyle choices all fall into place. To begin and sustain a loving, open and trustworthy relationship with yourself you must make time. Your priority is you. What can you do to set the stage for lovely activities with yourself? Some of my favourites are lighting candles, enjoying an epson salt bubble bath, listening to meditative music and journaling. Find what works for you and don't forget to spoil yourself often in loving, kind, heart-felt ways.

1. Solo travel

Have you ever gone on a trip by yourself? Maybe a road trip or a weekend away? If so, what did you learn about yourself during that time?

2. Teachers

Have you studied the work of any "gurus?" What speaks to you most in their teachings? What have you incorporated into your life as a result?

3. Habits

Have you ever eaten vegetarian or given up a habit, like smoking or drinking, that maybe wasn't the best for you? How did that make you feel?

Do you find it hard to stick with good habits? Why or why not?

4. Keeping a Record

Have you done any journaling around moments in your life that were either really hard or super inspiring? When's the last time you read them (maybe it's worth a read to see where you are at now)?

6

LANDING

NOW THE REAL WORK BEGINS.

Just when you think you've found it, it's gone as quick as it came. Love is like that. It's ever flowing, never something you get to hold onto... only memory remains.

After Ireland, coming back home had a whole new meaning for me.

It didn't matter where I was in the world, I knew how to come home to myself. I knew that everything I ever needed was within me. My happiness, fulfillment and joy were generated from deep within. There wasn't anything outside of me that could dictate these things. This was my gifted revelation, my truth. And I just knew it had to be the same for everyone on the planet as I now saw the world as one big living organism all playing into the game we construct as "reality."

I had full control on how I chose to live and whatever my circumstances would be, and this brought me great freedom. I no longer was swept away by the thought of "being someone special"… especially for someone else.

I had witnessed my own divinity. I already was Everything. GOD,

Supreme Being, Buddha, whatever you want to call it. This universal connection we all share made me feel unexplainable love. I had landed into a space within that I never wanted to leave. I wanted to live my life from this open and freeing place forever.

In any given moment I could see clearly how my thoughts, emotions and feelings were creating my world. How I had total control of my experience depending on what I chose to think about. That was the tricky part: maintaining control over what I thought about in any given moment. I was starting to see how that would become my life long practice.

In the meantime, liberation was mine. I could create whatever my heart desired from the place I was in.

Back when I had first moved to the city after high school, I had bought a workbook called *Putting your Talents to Work*. It was a sunny summer day, so I packed a little picnic and went to the park across the street to go through it. I was really curious to know what my talents were and what my purpose was.

What I discovered that day was that I loved helping people to do two things:

1. express or experience themselves at a deeper level
2. overcome a challenge or obstacle

Simply put, I loved helping someone achieve something big, something that pushed them into brand-new territory.

By that time, it had showed up in many arenas in my life ever since that time I'd convinced my dad to dance by the fireplace. That was the first time I'd ever gotten a glimpse of my purpose.

While I was still in Ireland, I'd journal about exciting career paths I could take once I arrived home. I envisioned hosting retreats where women could express themselves through movement and different forms of creative expression, connecting with their true essence. I wanted to *untame* the female mind, freeing it from domesticated thinking and opening it to a world of possibility and courageous action. I had tried something like this for teens during my improv training. I knew now that I wanted to specifically work with women to help them free their spirit. I found women to be my calling. It could have had something to do with the support and encouragement I received not only from my Mom but also the amazing women friends she had around her. They would always shine their light on my discouraged heart when times were hard.

But there were a few small hold-ups. I had no network and little to no experience, except for my own story. Also, coming home as a newly evolved/"woke" human had its challenges. I no longer resonated with my friend group or old way of life. I needed time to bring my visions to fruition. And I had it.

Before long, I was off on another grand adventure, something I had solidified over Skype in Ireland. I got a job as an emcee for the 2010 Winter Olympic Torch Relay across Canada as one of the Coca Cola team members.

Just under a hundred of us from all over Canada congregated in a hotel for non-stop four-day training to learn the ropes and team build. We all had our role to play in our travelling convoy. There were performers, acrobatic specialists, musicians, hotel coordinators, managers, Zamboni and truck drivers. The list was long. We were a travelling circus, basically. Along with some others, I was to be stationed on something that looked like a fire truck. It had a three-foot-wide platform around it so we could dance, sing and entertain the crowds as we passed them by. These trucks were loaded with pumping sound systems, flashy lights and safety railings. They also had two huge coolers on either side filled with cold

Coca Colas to hand out to all the people lining the streets. During our training blitz, we just had enough time to learn how to jump on and off the truck while it moved without getting hurt, learn what to say as emcees, get fitted for all our winter gear and meet our coworkers.

The magnitude of what we were about to do really didn't set in until we had our first run at it on Vancouver Island. We started there and then flew to Prince Edward Island. From there, we toured from city to city for over a hundred and six days until we reached Vancouver in time for the Opening Ceremonies.

We all were so excited to see our country in such depth over the next three months, every night in a new city, running the side streets, being hosted by different community centres and Indigenous nations. Everyone rolled out the red carpet for our arrival. The crowds would always stand in anticipation to get a look at the torch bearers—sometimes they would be famous people like Shania Twain or Sarah McLachlan—running with the Olympic Flame. It was most definitely one of the coolest experiences of my life.

Our job was to pump up the crowds, to get them in the zone to cheer, clap and wave to the torch bearers as they passed by. I feel like I high-fived almost every Canadian alive on that tour. When my voice needed a break from hyping up the crowd, I would hop onto the street and run. Our days were long. From six in the morning to nine at night we ran, walked, sang, danced and entertained the best we could, covering a total of forty-five thousand kilometres with breaks for lunch and the occasional re-position in the staff van.

Big cities were long-ass days with over three hundred torch bearers in a row. But some towns were quite small, with maybe six torch bearers. Those places would take about an hour or so to do. When we were done, we'd secure the truck by turning off the music and lights and hop in our van to drive to the next populated spot. There, we'd turn on the circus and do it all over again.

There was this one little town that only had one torch bearer. We stopped a few yards away from the crowd, got out of our van and got the truck ready to go with the lights and music. Then we entertained these kids standing outside of an elementary school holding their class-made posters reading "GO CANADA GO." When we were a few meters away from the school, we stopped, closed down shop and got back in the van, grumbling about our personal discomforts—hunger, cold, the need to pee—and took off. I glanced back at the kids, who were staring at us. One minute their faces were full of joy as they cheered with bottles of Coke in their hands, and now their expressions turned ultra-confused. They had gotten a peek behind the curtain of what reality actually was for us. Just a bunch of tired clowns.

We made sure we didn't make that mistake again.

This particular experience taught me that life isn't always what it seems on the outside. There are many stories running in the background of what might look like the most amazing experience of all time. Things aren't always as they appear! I'm always aware of that when judgement and comparison sneaks in.

Sometimes, the weather on that tour would reach twenty degrees below celsius. I had never experienced cold like that before. Some nights our eyelashes would have little snowflakes on them. Other nights the rain would be so bad it would take me hours to shake the chill and wet.

The bathroom situation was also a big problem. The relay didn't stop until it was lunch or we were finished for the day. At the start of the tour, in the rural parts of Vancouver Island, we would take cover in nearby bushes or sometimes in people's yards and then run to catch up with the truck down the road. But if you missed the truck, say because you ran into a Tim Hortons to grab a coffee or pee, you would have to wait for the hotel admin group to pick you up. They'd either take you to the parade route or to the new hotel for the night, depending on which was closer. The higher ups were always watching and they were never pleased if you got lost en route or missed your shift. I had two very close calls myself.

One happened on day five out of the one hundred and six we'd be on the road. My roommate and I thought we'd set our alarms and for whatever reason they didn't go off or we'd slept through them—who knows. We both woke up to hear the convoy leaving.

Ever missed the bus for school? This was like that, but worse as there's a slight chance the school bus driver will be nice and pull over for you. The relay, however, had no mercy.

We frantically put on our gear, packed our full-size suitcases and chased the trucks four blocks down the street with all our shit in tow. I didn't get to pee, brush my teeth or shower. It was a fuckin' hell of a day, but we just made it without anyone too important noticing, phew.

My other mishap happened at a lovely traditional territory museum. I got caught up chatting with the events person there. I was so fascinated with the history of the place that I totally blanked on the time. I noticed that everyone had left about thirty minutes later. I had to wait a few hours for the hotel admin folks to come by in their car and pick me up.

That was noticed.

One beautiful day in New Brunswick, I was on the top platform doing my emcee thang. I knew the President of Coca Cola was with us that day, so I was doing my utmost to be ravishing and remembered. I was walking around to the other side of the truck to entertain the folks there, microphone in hand, when I took a step and discovered that nothing was there to land on. I guess the last person who'd gone down the back stairs of the truck hadn't closed the hatch. I heard the microphone hit the top of the stair, making a "boof" sound, as I just barely caught the metal stair. My leg was throbbing and I was in shock, barely hanging onto to the platform for dear life. I was unable to move, yet I thought "The show must go on." I put the mic to my mouth with all the strength I had to muster and called out a few cheery phrases to introduce David, the other emcee. Then I started to cry.

I can't believe I just did this and the only person who saw what happened was the President.

He was behind the truck in his own decal-ed out car where he paged the truck driver to stop. I thought for sure I would be kicked off the team. I couldn't walk, run or even stand on my leg, and that was literally the job!

The traveling doc said it would be weeks before my ankle would heal and it had to be in a cast and I wasn't to put any pressure on it.

Way to go, Adera, you've blown it again.

But that didn't end up being the case. They decided I could stay due to the fact that I was great at the job. I just did my best to heal as fast as I could so I could get back into action.

I missed a portion of Quebec but was back on my game by Ontario. We had a team doctor who got me into good shape in a matter of weeks. I was thrilled the day I could take the mic and take it all the way home.

Every part of the journey, even the painful parts, were magic. The extreme experience my team and I went through created a bond I won't ever forget. And I think my attitude towards the whole tour was definitely influenced by the work I had done in Ireland.

Some people just couldn't hack it. It was tough. But my gratitude and fortitude saw me through.

When we finally got to Vancouver, we were relieved and really fucking tired. I basically slept through the entire Olympic Games. I didn't leave my dark suite for days. I made it out to a few of the parties but my body was done.

After a few weeks of laying on the couch, I decided to hit up Craigslist for work. There was a post for an intern position for a travel tv show that paid $600 a month. There weren't many other details except for the fact that this person would be responsible for coordinating and marketing the show. I'd heard of the man who hosted it, John Lovelace. He had been on TV for years with his other show, *Wings Over Canada*, so I knew this opportunity was legit. I still had a hankering for some limelight and TV cred.

I met with John and his two editors, assistant and cameraman, all of whom I worked hard to impress. I got the job. I had a few months to coast with the money I had saved during the relay, so I had nothing to lose and the opportunity to be on TV to gain.

It wasn't long before I was running the show. I was booking the guests, coordinating the locations and marketing the episodes on social media. John was pleased with my work and asked if I'd be interested in hosting some of the segments. *UM, YES PLEASE!!! YES, YES, YES!* I would get in the company car with my cameraman friend, Jason, a guy I had worked with back in my radio days, and travel across British Columbia to film segments together.

It was awesome. I was getting the hang of this "making your own TV show" thing… and I was also circling my purpose: helping people achieve something big and new.

A lot of the people we interviewed for the show had never been on TV before so I took great pride in making them feel comfortable and natural on set. I would hear: "I was so nervous but then you made it so easy. I didn't even know there was a camera." That was the highlight of the job for me. That, and being able to hear and share people's stories while visiting so many different locations. I loved to hear what people were passionate about and how they brought their passions to life.

One time we were up at Lake Okanagan filming a typical "walk and talk" piece. As we wrapped, I stared at the lake. Suddenly, this wild thought came out of nowhere.

The voice in my head said: *"This is where you'll get married."*

Wow, what? Where did that just come from…?

Huh, ok.

For a moment, I took it in and appreciated experiencing such a clear premonition. Then my rational mind kicked in and said, *You have no eligible suitor, so there's that.*

It was true. I had no idea when or how it would all come together. I just knew maybe one day it just might.

I had been producing and hosting the show for a year when I had to coordinate a hundred aircrafts to meet in the Yukon for a special fly-in show. After that, I started feeling a little frustrated with my lack of pay. I was barely making minimum wage.

Besides, I'm starting to understand how this all works. I could maybe do this!

First you had to get a network to agree to air your show. Then you had to find product placement, advertorial style spots or commercials to pay for the production costs. Now, this wasn't traditional TV by any means, but it was a way to make it on the cheap and it was a model that could potentially work for me.

On my next day off, I flew to CHEK TV in Victoria and sat down with the executives there, as that was one station that was airing our show. I pitched them my idea for a TV show: a mixture of sitcom humour and local business spotlights. To my complete and utter astonishment, they loved the idea and gave me an 8:00 p.m. time-slot on Thursdays.

That's the Friends *time-slot!? Holy shit! Could you imagine if my show got that big?!*

My head spun in ecstasy as I flew back to Vancouver to tell my other two partners: Jason the camera guy and Brian, his writer-actor friend.

My dream had come true. I was going to have my very own TV show!

Jesus Christ. Now I have to go make a show.

Questions to Free Your Spirit

This was a critical part in my life where I got to witness who I was around others and what I brought that was uniquely ME to the ring. I caught myself in a team setting, and in a leadership role and I got to see my strengths and weaknesses in both. It was a time to learn how to interact with all walks of life in a way that created connection and trust. I met a lot of new and diverse people during this time, and I loved interacting in a way that was respectful and honest and noticing when I could have done it better.

1. Outgrowing

Have you ever felt out of place with your old group of friends? Like you'd outgrown them or just weren't a fit any longer? What did you do?

2. Timing

Have you ever had a big vision for your life but knew the timing was off? Like you had to experience some things first before it could come to fruition? What did you do?

3. Stumbling & Falling

Have you ever let your team down before? How did you feel about yourself? What was your self-talk like?

4. Resting

Are you someone who can allow rest and rejuvenation into your life easily or are you go-go-go, push-push-push all the time? How do you feel when you finally stop for a while?

5. Risk

Ever done something really courageous like hop on a plane or declare your love to someone…and it worked out? How did that make you feel?

7

FUCK ME, THERE HE IS

When you're present in time doing what you love most, lost in your own created joy, life has the perfect way of presenting more of what you desire.

After our show was greenlit, I got to work making media kits and rate sheets. I sent out as many packages as I could to media outlets and companies alike, in hopes they would want to talk about or be featured on the show. Brian and Jason were in charge of writing the show, filming and editing. I was the one who had to bring in the business and the connections so I was up to bat first.

I would walk into any and all stores, restaurants and shops and cheerfully hand out our info. I'd highlight the potential benefits, talking up where the show would be seen, the kind of demographic we were attracting and how we proposed to promote it. I felt with conviction that this was an extraordinary and unique marketing opportunity for any local business.

I also had my eye on a few car dealerships to sponsor our company car, as I didn't want to travel in a granny-style '91 two-door Tercel. It didn't exactly say "high flying business woman."

Mini Cooper was my first choice. They were keen to have us at their next big launch party as long as we brought out our cameras. I needed a promo video and some teasers to send to CHEK, so we decided to go for it. We tried our best to win their hearts. But they ended up taking too long to make up their minds, so I went with my second choice, a KIA Soul.

For each show, we needed six companies to say "Yes." Once they were secured, Brian and Jason would get busy writing the episode, weaving humour and backstory between the business spotlights.

Now..what *exactly* was the show about, you ask?

Here's what we'd pitched to the network:

> Adera Angelucci is a motivated entrepreneur building a fresh new event planning business called the GO*to*GAL. Determined to make her young company a success, Adera is obliged to take on any and all clients. Whether it be a two-person engagement party or a one-hundred-invitee birthday for a seventy-seven year-old chihuahua, Adera is up for the challenge. Often provided inadequate time or budget, Adera seeks the unorthodox help of her long-time friend, Brian, and her bubbly assistant, Lindsay. Brian is a self-proclaimed actor with time on his hands and Lindsay has a gift for sniffing out a bargain. Together they deliver the city's best places, products and services to their client. Every episode provides an insight into the professional and personal life of this determined woman as she overcomes the challenges of her new occupation and strives to exceed her clients' expectations. Shot like a modern reality show (e.g., *Glutton for Punishment*, *Property Virgins*), GO*to*GAL provides a dynamic, on-the-go style, highlighting real places, products and services, blended with traditional, scripted sitcom scenes (e.g., *The Office*, *Modern Family*). This mix is sure to provide the information, entertainment and humor viewers are craving.

There you have it!

By the second month, thanks to my manic hustle, I was able to secure twelve businesses and we started filming. I was having the time of my life using my sales, marketing and promoting skills. I was meeting new people every day, hearing their stories and learning about their businesses and passions. I had cameras rolling, photos taken, media calling for interviews and I got to work with all my friends!

Life really couldn't be better. The only thing that weighed a tiny bit on my mind was that I was creeping up to thirty and had zero love prospects. Even though I had found my self-love, it didn't mean I wanted to be single forever. I still wanted an amazing partner in my life even if I didn't *need* him.

This was about the time I also discovered Kundalini Yoga and I was hooked!

The first class reminded me a little of my Sri Chinmoy experiences, which is why it didn't feel weird at first. The students wore white, had tea and biscuits (nice touch) after each class, and were vegetarians. They also worshipped an Indian dude named Yogi Bhajan and did a lot of chanting, breathing and meditating. This was not your typical yoga class, and that's what I dug about it.

This yoga tech is insanely powerful. Most classes, I would experience a full-on melt down, crying or wailing my old hurts out of my body. Or else I would have temper tantrums and get so angry that my whole body would vibrate as I let go of past resentments and "what if's." It was elating to actually work with the energy in my body and see it dissipate and transform through movement in this way. That was one thing that had been missing in the Sri Chinmoy meditations: repetitive, hard movements that make you come face to face with your inner resistance and then use the release to rewire the nervous system and actually create new pathways of consciousness.

I didn't know I still had pain in me to expel but it was clear from my classes I did. It felt so good to shake that shit off as I embarked on a new chapter, recalibrating myself for what my presence held.

Emotions can easily get all wound up in the system, causing dysfunction and disease. I recognized the importance of having tools to eliminate discomforts as they arose in the present or emerged from past experiences.

Who knew this technology would come just in time for what was about to unfold?

Feeling so damn good about life, I decided to take a chance on Plenty of Fish.

Lots of people I knew had success with online dating so I thought I'd give it a shot. Truthfully, I didn't want my love story to start with *"I clicked on his profile,"* but hey, if it's love, who am I to say how it arrives?

One night, I fished a handsome fellow who had his own successful business and was into yoga and travel. He sounded awesome on paper, so I was keen to meet him. *Could this actually be the one?*

After a few dates, I was starting to fall hard. He loved having deep meaningful conversations. He was super fun. And get this: He was good friends with my teenage salsa partner back in Mexico eighteen years ago. It was a wild reunion.

But there were a few red flags that I was having a hard time with. One: he would take forever to text or call me back. Sometimes it would take a few days. Two: he was always running late and forgetting that we were getting together. Three: his friends were more of a priority to him than me and told me that, straight up. When I would tell him these things weren't working for me, he wouldn't return my phone calls or texts.

Then, he just took the low road and disappeared completely. No closure, damnit. You can bet your ass I Kundalini'd the shit out of that one. I couldn't believe, after all the work I had done, that I would get such a dud fucker.

Brian and Jason had to hear about all my man turmoil with this jerk for a few solid months while we filmed the show. He did make me a little crazy.

The experience taught me that it's one thing to be cool with yourself and it's a whole other thing to be cool with yourself with another.

That was the work I still needed to do.

I'd heard *Calling in the One* was the go-to book for anyone who's ready to meet their soulmate so I picked up a copy.

I would read a bit each night and do the homework it requested.

Around the same time, Brian, Jason and I pulled off a crazy successful red carpet premiere party at a high-end waterfall venue downtown. I wore a sexy designer dress and we pulled up in a limo, looking to wow the who's who in media.

After the gala, we bunkered down, getting ready to deliver a full season of *GOtoGAL* to the network. The three of us plus an extra tv specialist editor blocked off the day to watch each show in detail to make sure there were no glitches or mistakes.

We were into our second hour by the time we got to Episode 3, which was about planning a dog shower for a wealthy woman. We watched a scene at a dog beach which included an actor friend of Brian's who played a creepy dog owner. I hadn't been there for the shoot, so it was the first time I saw this episode and the actor.

"Hold on, pause this," I said. "Who is this guy?"

"It's Ryan," said Brian. "Remember the guy I was telling you about who was cool to do the scene for us?"

"Yeah, yeah, I know that, but who *is* he?"

Everyone in the room was looking at me like, *what does she mean, "who is he?"*

"I mean, why didn't you tell me he was so cute?" I said. "I would have been there."

Brian was confused. "You wished you'd come because he's hot?"

"Yeah! You didn't tell me he was good looking. Is he single?"

Brian looked at me and at the other guys like, *is she serious right now? We have real work to do.*

"Yeah, he's single," Brian said, with a look of *can we get on with it now?* "But I don't think you guys would be good together."

"Why not?"

"Well… because he's super nice and you're…"

I was looking at him like *for the love of God spit it out, this guy is so cute...*

"You're a little crazyyyyy," he ended with a high pitched, sorry-to-be-the-bearer-of-bad-news voice.

I nodded. *Fair enough. He did just witness me go bonkers over this Plenty of Dead Fish Dude.*

I apologized to everyone for the hold up. But as much as I respected what Brian had to say, I still wanted to know more about this actor friend of his.

Ryan. The nice guy.

When I got home that evening, I found Ryan on Facebook and sent a message thanking him for being on the show. I said usually all our guest actors receive a box of chocolates from our sponsor and ask he if wanted to meet to get them and maybe have a beer as well?

Sly Adera.

He said yes, so I suggested we meet at a local bar that had an improv show that night. I thought that would be a great idea just in case we had nothing in common. That way we didn't have to sit there and talk to each other.

I arrived a few minutes early, so I ducked to the bathroom quickly just to get a final check on myself. I was nervous. I had creeped his Facebook pretty good so I thought I could tell what he was like, but you never do know.

As I swung open the bathroom door, Ryan was exiting the adjacent men's washroom. We basically bumped right into each other. After an awkward and startled "Hi!" "Hi!", I didn't know what to do—so I gave him a hug.

During that embrace, two thoughts went through my head:

1. Fuck, he's shorter than I thought.
2. I am going to love this guy for life.

After we pulled away from each other, I presented the chocolates.

"Thanks," he said.

"I will be right back! Just gonna run to the loo."

He nodded.

OMG, get a hold of yourself. He saw you just leaving the bathroom, what are you doing here again, you loser?! UGH. Holy shit, what did you get yourself into? Ooooh, this is going to be fun! Oh man, he's not what you expected. Oh geeee, you've never met anyone like him before and you can tell. Ahhhhh, here we go!

I walked out of the bathroom (again), trying to remain calm. I saw him chatting to a gal he obviously knew. I thought that was pretty cool. He introduced me to her and she gave me a surprised look like, *Oh, that's not who I expected.* I thought that was a little strange. Then she was giving us the vibe that she wanted to sit with us but somehow Ryan was able to maneuver us to the bar with no extra chairs so it would just be us.

We ordered two winter ales (it was also his fave beer besides Guinness). He explained to me that he and his ex-wife had split about six months earlier and he hadn't seen that friend for a year. He knew she didn't know they had separated, so that's why I got such a weird look.

Oh ok, cool, no worries. Married?? Mmm, I'm going to have to get more of this story.

The improv group wasn't in top form that night, so we enjoyed making side comments and jokes during the show. Ryan was funny.

There was also a horrible stench coming from the bar where he was sitting. I would get whiffs of it when I would lean in to tell him something. I was praying it wasn't him.

Once the show ended, we decided to go get a bite down the street and get to know each other better. I told him on our walk (a few drinks in at this point) that I'd thought he had a god-awful smell coming off of him but knew now that we were outside that it was just the bar. He had been worried that I thought it was him the whole time we were sitting there. We had a giggle about that.

We ordered pizza, more beers and talked about everything and anything. I made a complete fool of myself by dropping my napkin on the ground, then bending over to pick it up, forgetting that we had a high-top table. I completely wiped out on the floor, nudging the cocktail table over a few inches in the process. I popped right back up within seconds, assuring everyone around us that I was okay. That there was nothing to see here.

We laughed. I was drunk and he was still hanging in there. Soon, we were the last two in the restaurant.

At 2 a.m. the restaurant was closing, so we decided to go for a walk. We walked for an hour through the desolate side streets to the city beach. There, the still darkness struck us both as a bit eerie. We decided to walk back to his car. On the way, a coyote crossed our path and stared at us for what felt like a long time.

What does this mean? Is that trickster energy?

Maybe, if you're into Animal Oracle Cards as much as I am.

Coyotes—tricksters—remind us to have humility for life's twists and turns, and that things might not look as you think they should but they're exactly how they're meant to be.

I felt safe with Ryan, even though I refused to let him drive me home once we reached his car. I didn't want to have that awkward kiss goodnight or a *do you want to come in* type conversation. It was late and I wanted to assert my independence. He told me that he knew that was what I was doing and that it wasn't necessary. He said he was happy to just drop me off at home without any pretense. I gave him a hug, thanked him for the night and off I walked home. I was looking forward to talking to him again soon.

He texted me the next day and asked how I was feeling. It was the first time I had gotten a text the very next day! How divine.

We texted back and forth, and a few days later he asked if I wanted to catch some of a film festival and go for dinner.

I said absolutely.

We had a lovely date on Commercial Drive, and drank margaritas after the show. I only had a couple, so I would be in better form for our goodbye. When we got to that part, we leaned in for a hug and a nervous "thanks, buddy" came out of my mouth. I was really playing hard to get and not on purpose. I just really liked him and still wanted him to know I was independent. As I walked to my car, I looked back at him and he gave me a look like *oh, I'll show you "buddy."* I faced forward with a huge smirk on my face.

A few days passed while we texted. Then he asked me over for dinner.

When I got there, he was in the kitchen cooking up a storm. He poured me a glass of wine, asked me to sit down and asked how my day was. When I finished talking, he came right over to where I was sitting, stood me up and kissed me. It felt... loving.

As we pulled away, I said in shock, "Well, okay then, thank you." I smiled with relief.

He went back to making the meal, confident that he had broken the buddy barrier.

During dinner, I bit down on something crunchy that felt like it shouldn't have been in the chicken. I took it out of my mouth and saw that it was glass.

"What the fuck?" I said as I ran to the kitchen to spit out my mouthful. There I saw a shattered glass dish in the sink.

"There was glass in my chicken?!"

Ryan was so ashamed he didn't know what to say. He ran over to make sure I was OK.

"Oh my god, the dish broke after I took the chicken out but I didn't think there would be any glass in the food. It must have sprayed up onto the counter."

"So, you broke the glass in the sink?"

"Yes. It was hot and I accidentally ran cold water on it, But it was after the chicken was already on our plates so I thought it would be OK. Oh my god, I am so sorry!"

He was so mortified. He had tried so hard to make me this wonderful meal. In fact, I found out later he had had his buddies over the night before and prepared the exact same dish for them to be sure not to mess it up. Come on, how cute is that?

Too bad my worst nightmare happens to be getting glass in my throat or my eyes. GREAT.

Well, that killed the mood for eating, so I opened another bottle of wine and we dove into some good convo around our past relationships and childhoods. It was getting close to 2 a.m. again and I lived about forty minutes away, so I asked if he'd be OK if I slept on his couch.

"Don't be silly," he said. "You can sleep in my bed and I will sleep on the couch."

"No, *that's* silly. We can both sleep in the bed. I am just super tired."

"Of course! Why don't you go lay down and I'll clean up?"

So, I gave him another kiss and fell fast asleep in his sheets.

Which smelt awesome.

Questions to Free Your Spirit

1. Fulfillment

Did you ever have a job that you just loved? One that filled you with so much joy and excitement? If so, what was it and why did you love it?

2. Release

Have you found a technology for releasing past hurts or emotions that may be trapped inside? If so, what helps? What tools are in your tool kit when you are suffering?

3. Duped

Have you ever been duped? Ever thought you'd found the right guy but then it turns out that they're far from being your dream partner?

4. Intuition

Do you have premonitions? Like when your intuition kicks in and has future information for you? Like my "I'm going to love this guy for life."

5. Hard to Get

Have you ever played hard to get? If so, why did you choose to not give your love up so easily?

ADERA'S GUIDE TO KNOWING IF WHAT YOU HAVE IS REAL LOVE (RL) VS. INFATUATION-CRAZY-FIXATION LOVE (ICFL)

RL: Feels effortless and energetically equal.

ICFL: You worry and fret about whether they're going to text or call.

RL: They make you feel safe when you are together.

ICFL: You feel a bit uneasy or are aiming to please or are questioning your actions often.

RL: You take time to hear each other out when it comes to a difference of opinions.

ICFL: You shut the other person down, unwilling to hear their point of view.

RL: You make an effort to do lovely, thoughtful things for each other.

ICFL: You don't really think about doing things for each other OR one of you does too many things that the other person doesn't reciprocate.

RL: You look each other in the eyes when you're making love and when you say I LOVE YOU.

ICFL: There is rarely any heart-to-heart eye contact.

This was feeling like **Real Love**.

8

RELATIONSHIP

Loving someone takes acceptance, while letting someone love you without deliberately destroying it takes faith. Real love means you need to feel love and be love, which takes practice.

In the morning, Ryan and I had coffee and I headed home. We made plans to go on another date the following day. That was how our relationship bloomed. Lots of back-and-forth texting, always planning our next get-together, being there for one another and caring about each other's feelings while working out our differences. That's what made this partnership different.

These were things I hadn't experienced before, and it took some getting used to. I had to adapt to what a healthy relationship could look like. At first it was endearing and fun and I felt worthy of it. And then, as my feelings started to heighten so did my fears around trust.

Ryan had no trust issues in his past, so this was a *me* thing I had to sort out.

I moved into his place at the four-month mark even though I was still struggling to trust him fully. There was a thought that he might leave me for someone else so I had to stay on my toes, even though I had zero evidence of anything like that happening. I would reassure myself by looking through his phone, computer, and Facebook. My *crazyyyy* had come out to play.

Maybe Brian was right. Maybe I'm incapable of being with a loving, kind and nice man.

I was mortified by the way I was acting. And to make matters worse on the self-esteem front, GO*to*GAL was over.

The show had been airing for a few months. My partners and I were just so relieved that we'd been able to deliver! It was a lot of work, but we all were making very little. The problem was that I couldn't seem to sell spots appropriately. I was doing it the only way I knew how, but it never seemed like enough money was coming in.

It was quite a trip to see my mug on tv though. My childhood dream had come to life before my very eyes. It didn't look or feel at all like I had imagined it would. It wasn't glamorous, and I didn't feel important, notable, prestigious or wanted. But nonetheless, it was real. It *happened*. We didn't win any awards or accolades for our show, but we still celebrated the fact that as a team, the three of us could heave out such an epic project.

No one was to blame for the end. We all had our own reasons for it. We decided to quit making the show and go our separate ways.

I was super disappointed that I couldn't keep my childhood dream alive and that my partners and I didn't hold the same vision. I was questioning my leadership ability and if working with partners was the best way to go. It felt easier to go it alone, and not have other opinions to butt up against. But I had no idea what I could do on my own that would satisfy all my desires. And I was falling in love.

When we found our dream place on the beach a few months later, I finally hit rock bottom. I collapsed on the floor crying uncontrollably. I tried to explain that my abandonment issue was rearing its ugly head and I couldn't control the waves of emotions I was having.

Ryan met me on the floor. He cradled my sobbing face and looked me in the eyes and assured me that he wasn't going anywhere. That I had nothing to worry about and that my hurt inside could finally heal as it wasn't needed anymore.

I was safe. I was loved back.

I knew what we had was real, but I couldn't shake the fear that he would leave or that I would sabotage it so he would have to leave, just so I could say:

SEE, I TOLD YOU YOU WEREN'T GOING TO STICK AROUND. I KNEW IT!

My damn ego was running the show, tying my stomach in knots, but Ryan stayed the course as promised. Mine was a trust wound that couldn't be healed alone. It required a partner to work it through with. Ryan had his own share of self-doubt issues to work through, so we were of service to one another, growing stronger together.

We loved supporting each other's big dreams and desires. Since he didn't love his current job and I was looking for something new to do, I suggested we open a video and marketing company together. He had schooling and know-how in writing, filming, and editing and, well, we all know what my skill set is by now. So, we created SPIRO Creative Inc., a video-storytelling company that showcases awesome people, products and services.

The only challenge was, we only had $1,300 to invest, an older Mac laptop and we needed all the things one needs when starting a new business: Video equipment, a logo, website, marketing materials, business cards, subscriptions, emails, you name it. And we had zero clients. I reached out to GOtoGAL clients, offering them a discount, and within a few weeks, we were able to get all we needed to get started on a shoestring.

Ryan and I were and still are an amazing team. Anytime a challenge presented itself we were able to sort it out. I realized being an entrepreneur without a partner would be extremely difficult, as there are so many aspects to the job. It was and is a blessing to share the load with him. Plus, we had different skill sets, so we never got in each other's way. I knew how to do my role and he knew his, so we trusted the other to get the job done. He shared a similar work style to me, so we knew what to expect from the other which made the partnership grow.

By year three, we had won a few awards and were being asked to go all over the world to film people's videos. We knew how to work hard and also take time off to go on many travel adventures. Ryan surprised himself by actually really loving the cruise ship lifestyle, just as I knew he would. I myself discovered that I preferred being a passenger to a staff member, even though I enjoyed catching glimpses of the behind the scenes, fantasizing that maybe one day I'd go back to ships.

One of our cruises to the Caribbean held an unexpected surprise. Federico walked across the pool deck during sail away. I almost shit my pants. What were the odds that he still worked for the company and we'd be on his ship eight years later? We spent an hour catching up on one of the sea days while Ryan laid by the pool and read. Ryan taught me trust on so many levels. He never questioned my motives when I would hang out with other men. He trusted me completely, which was amazing to feel. That day reinforced the real love I shared with Ryan.

Ryan and I had simply created a beautiful, rich, romantic, adventurous, loving life together. We both felt truly blessed to have one another. The fact that we got to work and travel together was such a joy.

He's been the first guy I've loved who truly wanted me to be exactly who I am. And besides my hang-ups in the beginning and the fact that I nitpick about *house tidiness and the way in which cooking is done,* I want him to be exactly who he is too.

I had found my *Gerard.*

In fact, he's an Irish Scottish mix, no less. How fitting.

After Ryan and I had been together for a few years, I started to notice some complacent behaviours kicking in. Anyone who is in a long-term relationship knows what I am talking about.

When you live and work together for some time, it's not the same as it was in the beginning when you'd only see each other some days and each occasion you spent together was quality, with great conversations and frequent sexy times.

We recognized that it was really important that we keep the *fresh love alive.* We found that remembering what we absolutely adored about each other was a quick way to get there. Every day my calendar reminder would go off and it would read:

"Give Ryan a Shout out of Appreciation"

Ryan's love language is words of affirmation, so I try and let him know each day what he means to me amidst all the daily to-dos. Mine is acts of service in case you were wondering, and if you haven't read *The Five Love Languages* by Gary Chapman, it's a relationship must!

When I really need to dig deep on hard-to-show love days, I think about what life would be like without him. That quickly turns my mood around as I'm instantly reminded that I don't want to do this life journey without him in it.

I choose Ryan. And Ryan chooses me.

Here is a good exercise for gauging whether a person is a good fit for you:

Once you've decided what it is you are here to do, ask yourself, does your partner support you completely, and even work with you to achieve those dreams? And do you both share the same values?

Ryan and I checked all the boxes.

It was our third "when we met at the bar" anniversary. We'd been filming a wedding that night and didn't finish until 10:00 p.m. It was almost Halloween, and a friend of ours was having a costume party. We decided to sneak in for a quick hello on our way home, even though we were both so tired. I thought we should do at least one fun thing for our anniversary. We rolled up to our place around 11:00 and Ryan asked if I wanted to go for a walk on the boardwalk.

I responded with an over the top "NO! God, I'm way too tired for that!" but knew we should probably do something more. Then he asked: "Do you want to meditate together?"

He hadn't suggested that before (it was usually me). I thought that was really sweet, as he knew how much I loved to meditate.

As we got into our comfy clothes, Ryan suggested after the meditation we say what we loved about each other. Perfect.

After Ryan lit candles on my altar and got some pillows, we cozied in, listened to some peaceful music and took some deep breaths. We let go of the full day we'd just had and entered into the moment with each other.

We spent a few minutes being quiet and then we opened our eyes and I told him all the things I loved about him and how much he meant to me. When I finished, he gave me a kiss and asked me to close my eyes. He started telling me all the things he loved about me and our life and what it all meant to him. Then he picked up my hands and placed something heavy like a crystal in them, closing my fingers around it. *Is this an amethyst or something?*

When he was done, he told me to open my eyes. I looked at him with tears streaming down my face and gave him a kiss. I opened my palms and discovered the most gorgeous ring I had ever seen in my life. I couldn't believe it. It was perfect. He looked at me again and asked if I'd marry him. I said YES of course and he slipped the ring on my finger.

The engagement was so uniquely us. I just loved it.

Now we had a wedding to plan, and because I wanted to get married in May, we had six months to bring it all together. Good thing I knew where the venue would be. Wink, wink.

I had taken Ryan to Lake Okanagan Resort that summer just to show him the grounds and to see if he liked it there, hypothetically thinking *what if we did get married one day?* He liked it.

Come May, we invited our closest friends and family to a fun three-day wedding extravaganza like none I had ever attended— and Ryan and I had been to dozens because of our video company. The celebration, just like the engagement, was uniquely us.

We ran our own ceremony with consultation from a ceremony

guide I had known since I was little. We sat our guests in a semi-circle around us so they felt immersed in the experience. We didn't have a wedding party. I instead had seven goddesses who helped with certain aspects of the day, and when it came time to walk down the aisle, we went down together coming from different directions and then met up at the altar. We picked a song that you sing when you open your Kundalini practice to soundtrack the moment.

ONG NAMO GURU DEV NAMO, meaning: "I bow to divine wisdom. I bow to the divinity within."

Ryan and I stood there in front of all our loved ones and told stories around how we'd met and fallen in love. We read some letters we had written to one another in the earlier days as our rings were passed around and blessed by each person there. We had a few of our dear friends come up and share their thoughts on marriage and relationships. We laughed, cried and finally shared our vows as we placed our rings on one another.

When it came to declaring we were "husband and wife", we got all our guests to yell: "You are now sacred partners in life!" And then we kissed. Music played, we danced and took a big group photo with sparkling wine to commemorate the moment.

It was the most magical and exquisite moment of my life.

We ate under a canopy of twinkle lights, dancing in the wind and lip syncing to our favourite songs.

Ryan is my rock, and I am his wild river.

Questions to Free Your Spirit

1. Trust

Has the issue of trust ever been a concern in your relationships, whether with friends or a loved one? What did you do about it?

2. Messing Up

Have you ever gotten something you've always wanted, just to sabotage it in some way because you were scared?

3. Uniquely You

Are you able to deviate from the way in which "things are usually done" and create your own path? Are you confident in creating something your own way even though it goes against tradition or what people are used to?

4. Value

What do you value in life? Download my values list at www.aderangelucci.com and circle 4-5 that really resonate with you. Ask yourself if you are living out those values today, and with your partner.

5. Pros /Cons

Write a pros and cons list about your partner and with an open heart go through them together. If you can remain loving and light-hearted, it really is a telling and fun exercise.

9

LEADING WITH PURPOSE

Following your heart call doesn't mean there won't be pain. Hurt is a part
of life. It's how we choose to look at it that makes all the difference.

After a busy summer and a two-week honeymoon in Europe, we decided to add a fur baby to our family. Her name was Indy and she came from the streets of Tulum. I was the one who instigated the whole thing. Ryan wasn't sure we should make such a commitment with work being as busy as it was, but I thought it would force us to get outside, and that would be a good thing.

Then we had her. At first, I didn't know what I'd gotten myself into. Ryan fell in love with her at first sight. It was typical Adera and Ryan fashion: Ryan thinks before he makes decisions and Adera thinks after she's already made one.

There was no way Ryan would let me take her back, so I had to pull up my responsible pants (which I've always disliked wearing) and make it work.

Fortunately, Indy was truly the sweetest pup. From the start, she taught us so much about life. She had a few skin irritations which we tried to treat and somehow would always make worse. That drained our bank account until we found a magic pill that kept her itching at bay. She was my third dog (if you count Spirit) and I really hadn't had the best of luck being a guardian, so I was nervous and apprehensive about the whole thing. But Ryan showed me what it looked like to be a good parent.

We went on many fun family adventures together so Indy could run free. The Oregon Coast and BC's Caribou region were two of her favourites, places where she could run around with the other dogs, checking out all the wild life.

She had it good at home too. Every day, we'd go to the beach where she'd run through tide pools and frequently meet up with her best friend Townes. At least once a week, Townes' mom and I would bring a glass of vino to the beach, where we would sit on driftwood logs, watching the dogs be goofs for hours. I loved it as much as Indy! Hiking in the wilderness or playing in the sand all afternoon were things I craved more of, and with a dog, they became a priority. I could start to see how adding balance to my life was necessary. I couldn't be all work-work, travel-travel, social-social all the time.

With this balance, our business grew. Ryan and I started up an interview style tv show called Passionpreneur TV that aired on Telus Optik. I was building a solid network of women entrepreneurs who all inspired me and helped me to grow. I put on networking events and specialty workshops and still teach entrepreneurs how to be on camera confidently, and how to market themselves with ease. I love inspiring them to follow their passions and put them out there so people can see them.

I was a creative, passionate entrepreneur who hosted a web show, ran a production company, met awesome cool people and told their stories for a living and I'd been doing it for almost seven years. I couldn't help but think back to how it all began.

It really all came about by engaging in jobs where I could see my talent and skill at work. That was when I knew I was on the right path, following what felt good. In each job I had, whether I was waitressing, child-minding, binding books, retail sales, personal shopping or deli-counter assisting, I could see what I liked and didn't like to do. I knew I loved being around people and being of service. I knew I loved to help people with non-tangibles instead of products or physical services, I knew I wanted to make a difference in their lives. I loved when I saw someone do something that was outside of their comfort zone. I loved 'putting on a show', lighting people up with my antics or entertainment. I knew I had to do something different, out of the norm, and create in a way that would inspire me and challenge me daily. I knew I needed flexibility and a free lifestyle. I could take risks and remain open to any and all opportunities that could potentially lead to where I wanted to go.

I had to have the courage to ask for what I wanted when the call presented itself, and most importantly, manifest confidence by believing I brought value just by being myself. My confidence cultivated the inspired actions I took. And the more I trusted what I truly wanted and not what other people wanted of me or what mainstream success looked like, the more confident I became.

The more I stood up and did what felt right to me, the more I created new levels of existence.

I became aware of my innate presence and saw that I was capable of doing whatever I wanted. The question was always "what do I want now?" I would follow my internal compass for the answer.

That's what brought me there, to the place where I was creating my life with another person who fully saw and supported me and where I was building connections with other like-minded people who were also blazing their own trails to do what they love and help people the best way they knew how.

All of it took guts—and it still does.

On one of our video travel trips, Ryan and I accompanied a group of women on a soul stirring trip to Nicaragua. The group lead, Chantelle Adams, wanted each of the gals to have their own Soul Story video as a memento of the trip. Everyone would be pushed out of their comfort zone in some capacity throughout their time abroad, and that included me.

The remote lodge on the beach was super rustic. A family of bats decided that our room was their late-night shitting grounds. Mosquitoes were out for the taste of my blood, and water was to be used sparingly. I admit it, I'm a 5-star travel lover, so I was having a hard time just being there, let alone participating in the activities Chantelle had planned.

One day we hiked up an active volcano for two hours in the sweaty heat to go surfing down the other side. Fortunately, we had helpers carry our fifteen-pound boards. Poor Ryan was scaling the side of the mountain while holding his video camera, trying to get as much footage as possible in the thirty-six-degree heat and wind.

When we reached the top, the view was spectacular. You could almost see the whole country. We got into the overalls that were meant to protect us from the hot little lava rocks getting on our clothes, put bandanas over our faces and adjusted our goggles. We were supposed to go one at a time down one of the two paths that were the designated sledding routes.

The instructor told us that if we leaned back on the board it would go faster and if we leaned forward, it would slow. Seemed simple enough.

The first two women got into their places, sat on their boards and pushed off. One gal couldn't even get any speed because she was sitting too straight. The instructor had to run down the mountain and help her out. The other one was probably going about five kilometres an hour.

I didn't climb up a hotter than hell mountain just to sled down it at turtle speed. No SIRREE. I hopped on my board right where I was and decided to just go for it.

No path, no problem.

I couldn't understand why it wasn't a free for all. It was a freaking large-ass mountain of loose fine gravel with tons of space for everyone to just go it alone. I didn't get why we had to sled down a path. So, off I went. As soon as I started sliding down, I heard the instructor yell something in Spanish but I couldn't understand, plus I was committed to showing everyone how brilliant I was. I wasn't going to wait in the line when I could blaze my own trail!

As I picked up speed, I started getting hit in the face with what felt like big rocks. *Thank god for these googles!* To save me from the sling shot smacks, I leaned further back on my board. I hit warp speed. I couldn't see a fucking thing with the loose gravel spraying in all directions. I was barreling down this mountain blind hoping to Christ I wouldn't kill myself. I caught some screams and gasps as I flew past the turtles midway down the mountain on their safe, predictable paths.

I made it to the bottom in record time with my face intact and enough sand in my jumper to create a Zen garden. A couple of locals at the bottom asked if I was OK. When the girls finally got down the hill, they came over to see if I was alright too.

"Oh yeah, no problem," I said. "I thought I was gonna die, but other than that it was great!"

Turned out the instructor had yelled something along the lines of,

"Don't go down there! It's going to hurt!"

The reason for the two paths was that the bigger rocks had been cleared away so you could just sled over top of the finer dustier rocks.

Ah, makes sense.

I looked back to see if anyone was daring to take the new path I had carved, but the gals were lined up responsibly waiting for their turn. It represented my entrepreneurial journey and leadership style nicely.

I was learning that not everything I created, not everything I did, and not everything I thought, would be of benefit to others, or actually work out. And I had to be okay with that. Being a Free Spirit in my business and life meant I had to do ME whether I had followers or not.

It always felt better when I did. But when I didn't, I had to love and honor myself anyway for at least having the vagina to try.

Ryan and I decided to take a leap of faith and to buy a place on Vancouver Island, a two-hour ferry ride away from our mainland beach town and our business contacts. I was sure that my network was strong enough that we would still be asked to film even with the extra travel fee. I was craving more peace and the world I had created on the other side of the straight was busy. I needed space to create something new. I wanted time to write this book!

Then our Indy unexpectedly passed away. She was only four and a half. She died in the backseat of the car on the way to the vet.

She had been diagnosed with a heart disease a few months earlier while we were away on a cruise in the Canary Islands. The vet had said it may have had to do with the food we were feeding her—the food that was recommended to us by the dermatologist for her skin allergies. We were in shock and completely perplexed on how this could have happened so suddenly and tragically. Without any signs! It just didn't make any sense.

We were heartbroken. Our girl was gone.

When something really hard and out of the blue happens, it's hard not to take it personally. To not ask yourself: *Why me? What could I have done better? Why didn't I know?* Not having answers can drive you insane; it did for us for months. But the fact is that these twists and turns in life are meant to be our greatest teachers. It's so hard to reconcile ourselves with these experiences. But they do deliver life's most precious hard, painful truths.

Here's what Indy taught me in her passing:

- Dark fur on a white couch doesn't matter when it comes to love.
- Play and fight with a gentle fun heart.
- Show the ones you care about how much you love them, always.
- Help out the ones who are smaller and younger than you by showing them unconditional love.
- Be present and revel in each moment like it might be your last.
- Give all beings equal respect. They know more than you think and they all have a beautiful gift to give as long as you're open to receiving it.

Dogs can teach us so much, as can every other living thing. We just never know when our time comes, and I am so grateful that Indy was able to live her Free Spirit throughout her entire life.

Even with these unbelievable blessings, the ones that leave us permanently mark our hearts. They are meant to be remembered. These chosen few are now a part of our unique stories forever. They shape who we become by the emotional lessons they teach us, and by how we become more compassionate to ourselves and others when we experience loss.

When you feel pain, you are able to share in someone else's pain more easily. The same goes with all the other emotions, whether it's joy, anger, excitement, whatever. Don't cut yourself off from any of it. These are the connections that create deep bonds with others.

Living in a vulnerable and open state is the reason why we're all here. To respect, appreciate and acknowledge everyone else's journey. Every human has experienced hurt. It's up to each of us whether we choose to act out our pain or learn new ways to heal our suffering so we can live a life of purpose.

To me, purpose is the thing you were born to do while you are here on planet Earth. It's that special mark that you are here to make on the other hearts around you. I believe a person's purpose boils down to four possibilities. Do any of these ring true for you?

1. Help someone else have an experience of themselves.
2. Help someone else have more ease and grace in their life.
3. Help someone else overcome a challenge or obstacle.
4. Help someone understand something at a deeper level.

It's the way in which you express this purpose that brings the spark of YOU to life.

Before I knew it, I was hosting women's retreats. One had over forty women. I realized that my wild career dream to work with women in a retreat style setting had indeed come to life without me overanalyzing or grasping for it. It was like the universe was just unfolding as it needed to support my ultimate desires as they moved and flowed through me. This trust was something that I knew I had to embrace and create more of. I started to understand I would be taken care of no matter what.

One common concern among these brilliant small business owners who attended my retreats was becoming stagnant due to their inner self critics and demoralizing attitudes. They worried that somehow what they brought to the table wasn't good enough. That they needed to know more, be more. That what they had to share didn't really matter or make a difference.

I am 100% sure you can relate to this feeling of "not enough-ness".

My mom, who is a Body Centred Practitioner and Health Coach has a cool theory that the feeling of not enough-ness could partially be due to lack of nutrients in your body. If your body isn't getting the proper vitamins, minerals or nutritional support, your brain receives the message and interprets it as feeling like you're not enough. Could be…

I also know that a comment by someone who mattered to you could set you up for unworthiness thinking. Or maybe you did underperform once and you had to make a choice whether you wanted to work harder at it or let it go, as it might not be for you.

Not everything comes with great ease out of the gate. Otherwise, where would your opportunity to learn be? And if we're not learning, then what are we doing? Just trying to be perfect all over the place? What would we talk about and connect over? What would we have the pleasure of working out or changing?

I try to explain to the women who come to these conferences that sharing their not-enough-ness feeling is actually doing us all a huge favour. Especially if they're willing to shift over to believing that indeed they are more than enough, and sharing that enough-ness with the group. By flexing their ability to show people what they can actually do, they begin reaping the rewards of people's praise. They actually get the feedback that they are more than enough. That can start new momentum.

Like these women, you have to practice this process. Especially when what you have to share matters to your heart even if it hurts.

Questions to Free Your Spirit:

1. Gifts of Sorrow

What moments in your life brought you great pain or sorrow? In retrospect, what did those experiences or people gift you?

2. Playing the Fool

Have you ever taken the lead in a situation and maybe under-performed or attracted zero interest from followers? How did that make you feel? What did you learn?

3. Purpose Possibilities

Looking over the purpose possibilities (in this chapter), which one of the four most intrigues you? Here they are below:

- Help someone else have an experience of themselves.
- Help someone else have more ease and grace in their life.
- Help someone else overcome a challenge or obstacle.
- Help someone understand something at a deeper level.

4. True Spirit

Do you let yourself mess up or do you try and act *perfect* most days? What's the fear in letting your true (occasionally messy) spirit shine?

Adera's Steps to Leading With Purpose:

#1 Believe that what you want to do is possible. Don't let self doubt or criticism stop you from trying something new.

#2 Be aware of the mind games you play with yourself that undercut your purpose. Those voices in your head are powerful (In the next chapter, I will share which ones are which so you know who to believe).

#3 Do the inner work to clear your resistance. This includes sitting in your resistance to see what it has to say to you. Does it have any valid points? Usually when we are resisting something there is a big truth there that we are afraid to look at. Take some time to see what the fear actually is and if it's been made bigger than it needs to be.

#4 Take bold daring steps that feel uncertain and hope for the best. Confidence comes from inspired action, not thought, so if there's something you want to achieve you must make a tangible move. You can't just sit and think about it.

#5 Keep moving in the direction of your dreams with practices that support and ground you daily. This is key to seeing a shift in your present situation. Once you make space and explore your inner realm, you'll start to be gifted realizations and creative ideas that could ping you in the next right direction of your dreams.

#6 Keep shedding the layers of made-up stories you created about yourself so you can allow your emerging self to glow through. There's a bunch of BS we tell ourselves on the daily to keep ourselves caged. It's good to notice when you are doing this so you can either choose to stay safe or spread your wings and fly. You always have a choice.

10

BUSINESS IS SPIRITUAL. SO IS EVERYTHING ELSE.

Finding my love—the love for another and a love for what I do—has been the ultimate journey.

I feel like choosing entrepreneurship has been the ultimate journey in free-spiritness.

With it, you have an incredible responsibility to bring something miraculous and special to the world through business. It's putting all your gifts and talents out there and hoping to heck someone cares and wants to buy them. I never get to predict where life will take me in my business, but I trust in the belief that whatever I'm meant to do next will be revealed. I'm living in the moment, taking in what comes. I learn to follow my heart even as it evolves relentlessly, and it's been the perfect path for me to date.

That's why business is spiritual, as spiritual as any other part of (my) our life lives. I believe business is meant to teach us and help us to grow.

Falling into my sacred self is a journey that keeps on delivering new treasures. Just when I think I have come to a place of wholeness

ιg, life can throw me another fun curve ball. Some
seem to take years to overcome, such as old beliefs
ı't want to let go or don't know *how* to let go. And
ance and different modalities to help me move
liefs so I can replace them with new ones. Ones
ɯɑι ᵴᵤᵖᵖᵒɾι, ᵯᵒᵤrish and see me for all I am here to be.

It's important I remain open. Especially when I find something tugging at my heart that goes against what I've been taught or what others think. I remind myself that what I've been taught is only what someone else has known to be true for them. It may not be true for me, and that's okay. All of human consciousness has been built on people's opinions so why not throw mine in the mix?

Make it interesting.

After many years, I finally learned how to differentiate between the voices in my head. Turns out there are three of them.

My *head voice* keeps my day to day to-dos and checklists in order. It's a machine for productivity, forward motion and occasional unhelpful self-talk. Essentially, this voice is my ego and it thinks it knows all. It does not.

My *heart voice* is my body's voice and it is always trying to get my attention. *Come on, move your feet, feed me, be nice to me, love me.* It speaks up pretty loudly when I'm doing things it doesn't want to do. Or if I'm in a place I don't want to be. It's spot-on.

My *spirit voice* is the trusted and true companion that shows up in many ways. Like I could be walking along the beach, feet in the sand, and I get this connected feeling of aliveness and gratitude. That *feeling* is the spirit voice, and it's more than just words. This voice can also show up as powerful intuition. For example, it can whisper things like, "I should bring crackers to this party", to which my head voice says, "No one asked you to, and that's weird to just bring crackers" so I don't bring crackers. And then at the party the host says, "Shit, I forgot to buy crackers!" Yeah… trust that voice, Adera.

I think it's wild that there are over seven billion people on the planet, each with at least three inner voices, whether they're tapped into them or not. So that's at least twenty-one billion different worlds running all at the same time.

What kind of world are *you* creating? That's all up to the voices you listen to.

Just because I love myself doesn't mean I don't slip up sometimes and fall back into the darkness of the soul. But when a not-good-enough statement or an I-should-have comment or an I'm-not-worthy judgement arises, my self-love is the first step to bringing myself home.

Without that love, it could be possible to stay in a deep depression longer than necessary, causing me to miss out on my highest good and deeper potential. If I didn't love myself, I wouldn't know what real love felt like. And that's what we're being called to do now: love ourselves and others. It's the only way we'll heal the fragmentations that have formed over millennia.

Nowadays, we are all out for blood. It's me-versus-them, that's-mine-not-yours. For true prosperity to arise, we all must know that we are *enough* at a deeper level.

Imagine if everyone had their core needs met because they knew how to do that deeper work of asking the right questions, and we all had access to the resources to find answers. Just imagine the world we would live in.

It's the world I dream of.

I used to believe for a long time that the things I surrounded myself with would somehow hold my value, status and worth. Hence why I wanted to be famous. But any time I got close to attaining these things, the feeling of worthiness was fleeting. Even heartfelt, sincere validation from others—though it can help to build your confidence—is never completely consistent or trustworthy.

This is the truth: your worth comes from within.

So, when comparison mode hits, I ask myself why I'm looking for similarities or dissimilarities in the first place. Am I perhaps hunting for validation that I'm "objectively successful"? Am I looking for belonging, possibly? To know that I'm on the right track, like "they" presumably are?

But here's the thing: I'm meant to build community with all sorts of different people.

After all, you are not meant to spend time with exact copies of yourself, all of you obediently following the "right track." And how could "success" look the same for a truly diverse group of people? So, next time you are in a room with people who have obvious dissimilarities, know that you are in the right place. Together, you're all making the party interesting.

Also, we are not meant to jive and vibe with everyone? Of course, some circles of consciousness will not feel comfortable, but I encourage you to hang out in them and see how it feels to be left out - to feel out of place and to know that you are still ok and that you are still a magnificent being of light.

It took me a long time to learn how to do that myself. But I'm grateful I did. Whether I drove a '91 Tercel with a GO*to*GAL TV sticker from Vistaprint on the back or a limited addition Mini Cooper, I needed to be happy, joyful and present to nurture real prosperity.

By not skipping steps and fully owning the moment, I got to where I wanted to go, anchored in wisdom, knowledge and wholeness. When I dropped the shame for being who I innately was and just respected people for where they were at, I felt more inclined to act truthfully, and to let my freak flag fly. And that makes for a more diverse and creative world. Now, free-spiritedness is *my* version of leadership. Not the "putting on a show" persona that I cloaked myself in because I lacked trust in my abilities.

I now "put on a show" in a very different way. I do so with an inspired idea and then put into motion the help I'll need to bring it to life. I also ask myself, why am I doing it? If it's for my pure pleasure and delight rather than the need to impress or entertain other people, then I move forward.

When I attached myself to an identity as a big so-and-so, *or a this or that, or needing to be defined by something external,* I experienced stress and a nervous breakdown. But when I learned how to sustain my power, realizing I was already whole and complete just by being ME, my outer world could totally fall apart but my inner world would still feel calm and secure.

Of all the methodologies and technologies I chose to support myself in this growth, Kundalini Yoga has been the most important.

Kundalini has helped me to control my inner and outer temper tantrums and move through the stress I caused myself. Yoga (and there are many forms) shows us spaces of solitude and grace. When we're not on the mat we are able to access these states of being more easily, as we've trained the brain to go there many times before.

This is why my practice is so important. With it, I can build the stamina to be able to endure any circumstance that comes my way. Now, ten years into my practice plus teacher training, I can monitor my emotions when shit hits the fan.

Yoga also taught me how to love myself unconditionally, and get better at loving those around me, especially Mother Earth. As you explore more spiritual work—this is always the underlying fear of coming into this work—you inevitably change who you are by realizing deeply who you are not.

The word "spirit" hits a cord with me as it signifies something greater than myself: an energy force that we all share that is uniquely expressed through our particular natures.

I love when I get a glimpse of someone's true free spirit. I feel a completely kindred feeling when I see someone living out their talents and gifts through their body. I can connect with them. I can see them. And most importantly, I can see love expressed through them.

It's absolutely magical to witness and feel. How have you felt when someone's essence shines? What is your experience when they are being their true self, showing their true light by being humble, real and present? Or displaying their talents in such a way that it evokes an emotion in you?

I feel that presence all the time in nature too. I am taken with its awe and raw beauty. Its spirit. Its energy that we all share in.

I believe there is a higher calling in each of us asking us to take the driver's seat in our own lives. To work with others in a way that's uncomfortable and new and different in order to create something meaningful and powerful for the betterment of all. To drop our judgements and preconceived notions and allow our creativity to soar.

You have your own ideas and your own way of seeing life. And you have a deep desire to see some of these ideas and ways of being come to reality, right?

You are probably creating something this very instant. You just can't help yourself.

Because you are a FREE SPIRIT, a leader. In your own life, in your own way of expressing yourself, in your own innate wisdom from the experiences you've had.

If you're ready to dive in and take your FREE SPIRIT nature by the reins, the first step is to get to know yourself deeply. All your habits, fears, beliefs, thoughts, instincts, memories. You are a universe just waiting to be explored, so keep journaling, keep your awareness alert and most importantly, enjoy all of your life's little and large encounters. They make up the footprints of your unique existence. Someone, someday, might really need to follow in those footsteps.

I know. You're on it.

I couldn't have imagined that my (frequently chaotic) experiences would lead me to where I always dreamed of going. Asking bus driver man on a date, or landing on a beach full of penises or hanging upside down off a Coca-Cola truck didn't exactly say "Hey, this way to landing your own TV Show!" But what I've come to learn is each unique experience that you engage in evolves the self to the next stage of life. If I had sat on the sidelines of life with a predictable job and home life I firmly believe I would NOT be where I am today. And that's a good thing, as I love who I am and where I am. Nothing in life is permanent, not even the markers. So, I took chances, showed my cards easily, got out there and met a whack of people. I created relationships and allowed those connections to guide my next steps.

Bus Driver man taught me to listen to that aching voice within that was too afraid to be truthful.

Penis Beach taught me to look where I'm going and to spend more time learning a new skill before reverting to my fearlessly cocky self.

Missing a step on the Coca-Cola truck taught me not to worry about impressing people, that my own safety and worthiness far surpasses what any VP would think of me.

I could go on and on with each of the stories, as they all lead me down my unique path. One I could have never predicted.

Today, I get to live my true purpose every day of helping people create and be more of who they are in their work and beyond. This is how I put it: "Make It Your Business to Lead with your Light"—essentially your *spirit*.

I've found my unique expression and now I help others find theirs by asking lots of questions.

It's amazing what you learn about someone when you ask them "what lights you up?"

That's usually their spirit talking.

More and more humans tapping into this way of being will shift our world totally. We'll stop focusing on what really doesn't mean squat and be totally in the groove with our purpose and ultimate power. We just have to believe and take inspired action steps towards what we truly want and fuck fear in the face over and over again.

Today, as I write this, I have a little being inside my belly. A new free spirit ready to take flight.

For that child, and for you as well, I make this personal declaration. You can make it too.

The world needs me now to stand up and claim my uniqueness.

I will invest in myself and the things that light me up.

I will feel full and whole just by being me.

I have nothing to prove.

I am on a mission to share what is in my heart however that shows up.

I am open.

My spirit is free.

Questions to Free Your Spirit

1. Judgement

How have you judged your surroundings? Are there certain things that people do that make you feel unsafe or outside your comfort zone?

How do you react? Think of a time you went somewhere or saw something that got your judgement to boil up. Did you retreat or pull back from the situation? Did you engage in conflict? How did that go?

2. Wildest Dream

If you were to really give it a go, what would you do?

Would you change careers? Start singing? Be a chef? Create a business? Buy a property? Tell someone you love them?

If you need any help with the above business endeavours, I'm here for you! You can check out my free content and other services at aderaangelucci.com. I look forward to hearing your story and working out a strategy to lead with your light.

MEET ADERA

Adera Angelucci is a Light Leader working with business leaders who need help with marketing and spiritual strategy. She's an award-winning producer, director and host with the video company she runs with her husband Ryan, SPIRO Creative Inc.. Together they have told over 2,500 stories. She also teaches Kundalini Yoga and meditation. Her favourite thing to do is gather a soulful group of women to strategize how they can reach their highest purpose.

APPRECIATION

I want to thank first and foremost my amazing partner in life, Ryan Smith. He has been my rock throughout my wild river of a life. He sees me, respects me and cherishes me, even though I can be a complete fuck up at times. I want to give sincere gratitude to his stillness and strength when I'm riding the waves of uncertainty or conjuring up my latest creative endeavour.

I'm forever grateful for my biggest fan, my Mom, Karen. She has always supported me, and even when she didn't like what I was up to, was never afraid to show her love. It's made all the difference.

My Dad, Larry, has always been my safety net. He's never shied away from lending a hand or pulling me out of a rough patch. He's been the voice of reason, and through the sarcasm and nonchalant exterior, he has the most compassionate and loving heart, especially when it comes to his family.

A huge shout out to all who love and care about me: my family, my in-laws, my mentors, my teachers, and my friends (You know who you are). You allow me to be me, and goodness, we sure have fun. The impromptu dance parties, late night deep convos and travel adventures keep us connected, and I love you as much as you love me.

My Sister Robyn deserves a special little note here. She has always given me such an accepting, loving place to land. Many nights, I've come crying or stressed, and she always had a way of listening and offering up sage advise that would get me through. I cherish our bond and all the ways she's gifted me wisdom throughout the years.

Also my epic editor Kristin, the undisputed bad bitch of the world (her words) who helped me bring my story to these pages. You complete me.

Thank you so very much to all my proof readers and endorsers. Your time and energy is greatly valued, and I appreciate your attention to detail and feedback to bring this book to print.

A special shoutout to Pamela Lynch for helping me through my sacred writing process, and to my dog Scout for being a fun, sweet, healing presence when I needed it the most.

Manufactured by Amazon.ca
Bolton, ON